Jack D

THE ANTI-CANCER MARRIAGE

Also by the author
The Causes and Prevention of Cancer

THE ANTI-CANCER MARRIAGE

Living Longer Through Loving

Dr. Frederick B. Levenson

STEIN AND DAY/*Publishers*/New York

First published in 1987
Copyright © 1987 by Frederick B. Levenson
All rights reserved, Stein and Day, Incorporated
Designed by Louis A. Ditizio
Printed in the United States of America
STEIN AND DAY/*Publishers*
Scarborough House
Briarcliff Manor, NY 10510

Library of Congress Cataloging-in-Publication Data

Levenson, Frederick B.
  The anti-cancer marriage.

  1. Marriage. 2. Cancer—Prevention—Psychological
aspects. 3. Cancer—Prevention—Social aspects.
I. Title. [DNLM: 1. Marriage—popular works.
2. Neoplasms—prevention & control—popular works.
QZ 201 L657a]
HQ734.L468   1987   306.8′1   86-42782
ISBN 0-8128-3127-6

To accept love requires taking the ultimate risk.
To the woman who always makes the risk worth taking.

CONTENTS

THE
ANTI-
CANCER
MARRIAGE

PREFACE

When we think of present-day cancer research, unfortunately we can easily picture the answers to our still unanswered questions as hidden on the other side of a large, tightly locked door. If we choose to imagine such a passageway to the answers to cancer's puzzlements, the door must certainly have some definite characteristics. First it must be old, it must be as old as antiquity, for that is how long mankind has been searching. Perhaps it should be constructed out of thick, heavy, dark wood with indecipherable carvings at the top center. They should be easy to see but unfortunately not within our ability to comprehend. At one time, a time before all of our close-to-useless technological advances, a time before the breakdown of the basic unit of human existence—the family—a time before cancer rates were considered epidemic, perhaps then these mystical markings could have been deciphered.

The lock soon gains our attention because obviously we must somehow have the proper key to permit access. As we try one key after another, as we try for generations to put together the precise constellation of grooves and ridges, more through a process of elimination than actually considering what we already know, we

11

never seem to achieve the correct pattern. Some master locksmiths suggest that the first ridge should be the one based on the study of cancer-causing substances (carcinogens).

These experts have placed onto this ridge on the key exposure to pollution, X rays, cigarette smoke, dioxin, and so forth. And then we encounter in the first groove, the two-pack-a-day smoker who lives to ninety, never developing a cancer. Slightly deeper in the groove is the individual who never had a cigarette touch his lips and succumbs to lung cancer after living forty years in a nonpolluted environment. Perhaps he even avoided being around others who smoked. In the same groove, we encounter the asbestos worker who after twenty years of such employment is still cancer free. The groove gets even more cluttered as another individual develops a malignancy after two months at such a job. The key easily enters when we consider the effects of such physical and chemical irritants as these. However, it abruptly stops at this first groove of massive contradictions. But because we wish to blame something outside of ourselves, we persist trying vigorously or gently to maneuver the key to force it to work. Whatever finesse we use we still fail in our useless exercise.

And then the experts from the nutritional field create a gentle ridge and carefully cut groove. The areas of the world where red meat and fat are readily consumed without resultant gastrointestinal or breast cancer become the massive rough next ridge. The key abruptly halts. But again, we keep trying. False totem or not, the comfort we get from our sense of control has us twisting the key with an almost fanatic determination.

And then the locksmiths of the mind make their noble attempt. Stress becomes one of the early ridges. The more a person is placed in such an environment the more these experts see a risk. As large and as obvious as this ridge is, its groove is equally deep. The groove of contradiction is present as soon as we encounter the top level corporate executive who for forty-five years has been

12

immersed in stress. The stress is removed with retirement to eighteen holes or largemouth bass, and within two years a tumor is detected. Some other locksmiths with an appreciation of the mind's influence over the body try to correlate worry, depression, loss, anger, and grief with a causal ridge or groove, but inconclusive test results create the obstruction that stops the key every time.

Virology has not so much as even picked the proper size or shape for the key to be ground from. Since 1909, when a virus was found to induce a connective tissue cancer spore in fowl called Rous sarcoma, medical researchers have been looking for a virus to explain all the different types of human cancers. Millions of man-hours and millions of dollars have been spent worldwide looking for a virus for lung, breast, bone, etc., cancer. We have found none since 1909. The evidence, even for leukemia, is close to nonexistent.

When we began a search for an AIDS virus it took only a few years of applying computer analysis to isolate the virus. That is because a virus was there to be found. Not even a first ridge or groove has evolved from the field of human virology in cancer research.

Perhaps the most pessimistic of locksmiths are those who insist on equating the cause of cancer with genetics. The first and most powerful ridge is cut from cancer's apparent propensity to "run in families." But in the groove we find that many personality traits are learned very early in life. And then there are the identical twin studies in the realm of cancer research. Identical twins almost never both get cancer, but if they do, they are almost always different cancers. If cancer were hereditary this would certainly not be the case.

In this same groove also rests one of the most powerful contradictions to the insidious hopelessness of cancer being hereditary. Divorced and widowed women in America and Great Britain are far more likely to develop breast cancer than married women.

There is no place on the hereditary ridge that states that there exists a gene for losing one's spouse at age forty to divorce or death. And yet, perhaps because heredity is so magical a concept, this useless and even hurtful key, while being stopped without even entering the lock, has applied more and more force year after year. This is a direct result of the frustrations we face due to the lack of real progress in cancer research.

Perhaps now we can decide how to grind our key more carefully out of the knowledge of the failures of the preceding attempts. And once we decide to learn from the works of the previous locksmiths a common unifying factor emerges. All of the grooves and all of the ridges are really based upon an individual's vulnerability to irritation. Irritation, whether it be nutritional, environmental, chemical, or emotional can be seen as the ridge, as the cause of cancers. And the individual's manner of processing irritation is the real groove in our key. How the person gets set up to do this processing is the most critically important factor in having the key not only enter but actually turn. It will explain why the heavy smoker may not get lung cancer and the non-smoker very well might. It will explain why one twin and almost never the other contracts cancer. It will explain why divorced and widowed women are at greater risk than married women. A theory that permits us to address these contradictions successfully can now evolve.

First we must clearly state what we do know from the realm of scientific research. We may begin by defining cancer. Any rapid and random growth that has no real purpose is cancerous. When we are sick, our blood's white cells increase in number to help fight the infection. When we break a bone the cells reproduce very rapidly to aid in the mending process. When we are infants, children, adolescents, or in a state of pregnancy we have fantastically rapid growth due to cell reproduction. None of these examples is cancerous. But when we have no such reasons for cells to reproduce so rapidly, when the organs have all been formed,

14

when healing is not occurring, such rapid growth has no purpose and no place to go. Instead we then see the formation of tumors or superfluous white cells as in leukemia and lymphoma. Cancer is a rapid and apparently random reproduction of cells. Cancer is a reactivation of infantile growth at the wrong time and wrong place. Cancer is the activation of a misguided, inappropriate healing process. We can view cancer as any and all of these.

To go any deeper in our biological understanding we must visit the research laboratory. The microscope becomes our means of entering the core of the cancer cell. The regulating mechanisms, even the ones that determine when and how the cell will reproduce or divide, are stored within the genes. It is the genes we must study carefully and thoroughly. And it is the genes that have already been sufficiently studied to answer enough of our questions to direct a significant part of the grinding process. It is enough to say that in every cancer ever studied the genetic structures are unstable. In numerous types of cancers the genes have actually been shown to shift position. Somehow this instability causes the cell to start reproducing much in the way cells reproduce in newborns. Cancer cells reproduce at the same rate as newborn baby cells. Cancer has growth hormones similar or identical to the hormone levels in newborn babies' tissues. If we follow this clue, the pattern of our key gets almost totally completed as we go back to examine what may have happened in infancy to make a person more vulnerable later in life. All of the unanswered questions of cancer can be answered if we just consider the significance of this stage—earliest infancy.

When a baby is born he is the essence of human sensitivity. Noise, light, smell, taste, touch, and loss of support, if sudden or sufficiently harsh, will all result in a startle reflex. The baby's ability to be irritated is at the highest level it will experience throughout its life. This bundle of rawness needs protection from external irritants as well as the biochemical irritants that hunger, growth hormones, and adrenaline-based reactions can cause. Almost everyone knows not to expose a newborn to loud noises, bright lights, temperature extremes, chemicals, spicy foods, cigarette smoke, or X rays. And almost everyone knows that hungry, wet, or cranky babies need to be comforted and soothed. Most people do not, however, consider that rapid cell division and growth may in itself be very irritating. As a bone mends in an adult fracture, the healing process, again due to rapid cell division, is very often painful. In the infant, growth is like a healing process in almost every organ system in the body.

How we respond to the irritated newborn will start a lifetime orientation of how internal and external irritation will be processed by the nervous system. In order for irritation to result in cancer it must change a vulnerable cell just enough, not to kill it but instead to trigger useless growth. In order for irritation to result in cancer, the cell must be predisposed. In other words, cancer is a multistage disorder. The first stage must happen, according to my theory, in early infancy. In order for the cells to get set up, certain events must take place. And in order for the later addition of irritation to take place certain conditioning of the nervous system must take place in the newborn.

When a woman is pregnant she becomes progressively more sensitive as her abdomen enlarges, her fears increase, and her awareness of a loss of control dominates her psychology. In the first trimester, she experiences a sudden hypersensitivity to smells and tastes. Things that she liked before she may now be repulsed, even nauseated, by. In the second trimester, the abdomen enlarges, and she becomes aware that there is no turning back. Mood swings and further increases of levels of irritability take place. She may also experience muscular discomfort. And by the third trimester, the mother-to-be, who we hope is very happy, is also very vulnerable and even more sensitive to all kinds of physical and chemical irritations. Fear of childbirth gets more and more pronounced. Muscular discomfort is at its worst as lower back, abdominal, and thigh muscles are strained under the burden they carry. If the mother-to-be is in a loving marriage and perhaps has women relatives or friends to support her, she will feel safe about all of the feelings that pregnancy induces. She may go through powerful mood swings. Tears may flow for no apparent reason. Feelings of dissociation, "spacing out," will frequently be present. And the more she goes through this reawakening of very powerful yet infantile feelings the better. Her nervous system and her biology are becoming more and more like that of a baby's. At the time of birth she will be in the most vulnerable and hypersensitive position any adult human being can experience. At the time of birth her baby will be in the most vulnerable and hypersensitive position any human being can *ever* experience. This similarity of nervous systems and biology permit an instant, overwhelmingly powerful bonding between mother and newborn. They continue to be one and the same. All the feelings, all the increases of sensitivity, all the fears during pregnancy are for a purpose—to facilitate this mother-infant fusion.

This fusion or bonding permits the mother to be unconditionally accepting of her baby. And when the baby is hyperirritated from internal (hunger, the need to eliminate) or external (noise, temperatures, caustic smells) stimulation, mother will be there to siphon off this level of overwhelming irritation. Baby then settles down. This means that baby's biochemistry changes from a fight-or-flight reaction to a peaceful, tranquil one. While all these normal reactions are happening, the infant's cells are reproducing at a fantastic rate in almost all body tissues. The only other time such a growth rate occurs is in cancerous growth later in life.

But if the mother is not supported by a loving husband and a close extended family, the baby will be placed in serious jeopardy. Mother is not at fault; her inadequate support systems are. This time when baby gets normally hyperirritated mother may at first be unconditionally loving, but after the third or fourth time she is awakened in the middle of the night, she may very well be anything but. Her husband is continuing to sleep, and she is hyperirritated at this point. The baby can feel her feelings—that is part of the mother-infant fusion. They both can feel each other's feelings. So mother is now bringing her irritation to an already hyperirritated infant. Instead of siphoning off the biochemical irritants, she is actually adding to them. At that very instant an excess of adrenaline-based reactions is taking place as cells are continuing to divide rapidly. In a lung, colon, bone, whatever, the dividing cells are exposed to excesses in biochemical internal carcinogens. As the genetic material reproduces and divides, a slight shift may occur under this chemical influence. The cell divides, but is now programmed to be unstable in the face of future irritation. A land mine has been laid down making the cell "precancerous." When mother calms down, or the chemistry just dissipates, the cells divide normally. The land mine is thus buried in healthy tissue. We can now stain and locate these land mines in living people. Unfortunately we can still not selectively destroy them.

At the same time these cellular changes are taking place, the nervous system of the baby is being conditioned. It is being taught to assume that being cared for is somehow dangerous. It is being taught to be overly concerned about the reactions of others. It is being taught to push away from intimacy, to actually fear closeness. And it is being taught to seek control in relationships to avoid being overwhelmed by the irritations others are viewed as inevitably providing. The "precancerous" personality cannot get established without cellular change taking place simultaneously. No mother can totally prevent some of these traits and some cells from being affected. If the traits of worry, depression, performance anxiety are powerful, it is safe to assume that many land mines have been laid down. If the person has a history of hypersensitivity to chemical and physical irritations, such as powerful early allergiclike reactions, we must suspect the physiology has been taught to be hypersensitive. But if the person accepts the foibles of life, seeks to be with others when depressed or irritated, and is not always trying to prove something, it is a safe bet that fewer of these land mines will be found.

Along with these precancerous characteristics already mentioned comes the most fascinating one. People suffering from such traits will also need to be irritated in order to feel calm. There is nothing in a cigarette that should calm anyone. It is loaded with irritating poisons, and yet we have all heard smokers under emotional duress say how desperately they need a cigarette. What they are saying is, "I need irritation to be added to my irritated present state." If mother represented survival, and if she brought irritation to the already hyperirritated baby, then we see a repetition of what is familiar when people light up. It is obvious that it is not what is best for any of us but rather what is familiar that motivates us. So the precancerous individual will also unconsciously seek out irritation in the face of preexisting irritation. This is how the nervous system got imprinted at the very beginning of life, and it is how the person clings to what is familiar. It has nothing to do with intelligence or even reasoning. It precedes such advanced concepts. The need for irritation to permit calming is part of the realm of emotions. It is an overwhelmingly powerful compulsion that is well beyond the ability of logic to control. The precancerous individual will be an irritation addict. All addicts know that their addictions—food, alcohol, heroin, work, worry, promiscuity—are not what is best for them. The need for the addiction, based on the familiar, wins out almost every time. The nature of the mother-infant bond and the imprinting it causes within the nervous system is the most powerful learning we will ever experience. It is learning on a totally involuntary, unconscious level. It is the foundation of personality.

Once the infantile cellular changes have happened we presently have no means of correcting the damage. But we can diminish the risk of cancer by recognizing our addiction to irritation and doing something about it. When we do, we change the level of *internal carcinogens* our minds and bodies produce. When we do, we reduce the cumulative effect of adding external carcinogens to the internal. We stop seeking the external and we reduce the production of the internal. The land mines from the first stage of life are much less likely to get stepped on.

Along with an addiction to irritation, an overwhelmingly powerful emotional orientation toward life is being learned at this earliest stage of development. People who will later personally confront cancer are unable to accept intimacy and caring comfortably from others. This type of infantile depression takes the form of pushing away in the face of human involvement. In the event that the individual who is so conditioned can remain in control, the closeness can be safe. Victims of malignancy are very comfortable with caring for others. They are horribly uncomfortable with being loved or cared for.

The best possible way of reeducating an individual's nervous system to reduce production of internal carcinogens is through a successful, loving, sexual, intimate marriage. The rest of this book will explain why this works. It will show how this can be accomplished through the fusion and bonding a good marriage should provide. It will show how marital bonding can be a repetition of the maternal-infant bonding, the bonding that should be the most protective in life. And it will show how and why this intimacy and sense of belonging in adulthood takes precedence over all carcinogen, nutritional, hereditary, and viral theories. It will show why married people outlive single people throughout the world. And it will show how destruction of marriage and the family is the most carcinogenic factor in modern societies.

When you turn this page you will have picked up the key. To answer all the questions that remain unanswered is now possible if we look to infancy and its long-term ramifications on how a person relates to others throughout life. We can now integrate *all*

20

the known biological facts with *all* the known psychological findings. Be skeptical, perhaps frightened, but use this key. It cannot hurt you or your loved ones. There are no negative side effects, only a real chance of protection for you and those you care about. Push the door gently, slowly, but make sure you know what lies on the other side. It starts on the next page.

1

A Fine Mess

"IT WAS DIFFERENT. WITH Bobby I felt really excited, like something special was happening. Josh did the same things, you know. He licked my ear and touched me softly. It felt sort of okay, but it's not the same. Maybe it's because Bobby was the first. I told you I went all the way with him after seven months of going out. I mean, I enjoyed it with Josh, but I didn't really. Something was not there that was with Bobby. Josh was really cute. He's tall and has blue eyes and sandy blond hair. And boy is he big! He's got muscles on top of his muscles. But when he kissed me it felt sloppy and wet. When Bobby kissed me it was wet and wonderful. I couldn't keep my hands off of him. We never let go when we were out together. Our friends used to tease us about Krazy-Glue and being Siamese Twins. When we hugged and made love, I felt like I was going to die, it was that good. All I wanted to do was melt into him.

"It was weird, but I remember feeling that I couldn't get close enough. We would lie back afterward and cry. Both of us. I guess I was crying because I was so scared of ever losing him. I began to worry about dying. Not that I was afraid of it. I was afraid of having to lose him. I tried to picture heaven without him and my insides fell out.

"One night on the beach I told him all this. He hugged me and started to cry. Bobby said he was afraid of the same thing and that if a god really exists he'd never let us spend forever without each other. I loved him more than anything in my life. I was seventeen. That's why I don't understand it. I was only away for the first two months of college. Josh was in my computer sciences course. I was a hotel management major. He was gorgeous. I forgot Bobby existed the minute Josh smiled at me. Those eyes, Paul Newman eyes. I can't figure it though because that morning I got another letter from Bobby. I started getting excited by reading it. When I went to class I still felt that way. Maybe that's why I was so vulnerable to Josh. But I mean how many married women would pass up Tom Selleck even if they were happily married? Especially if there was no way their husbands could ever know. This guy was better looking than any movie star. I mean a hunk, a fox, just gorgeous. We went out to the local disco-bar place. I guess I got a little too drunk.

"I didn't care that my roommates knew. Cathy was already dating someone besides her guy at home. Cindy had to lose forty pounds before she had anything to worry about. I mean she is cute, she has a real pretty face, but like my Dad would say, she'd win in a head-on with a Sherman tank. So I didn't care what they thought. Well I guess I was feeling a little stupid after all the raving I did about Bobby. But Cathy did the same thing. Then again she said she had lots of guys in high school and she did everything.

"Anyway, you should have seen their jaws drop when Josh came over in his Corvette to pick me up. They immediately understood what I was up against. I could tell they wanted to be up against it too. . . . Well I was when he went to open my side of the car, he pressed himself against me and kissed me real deep. I didn't push away, but I could tell immediately something was not right. I mean I knew I'd go all the way, and it was exciting, but just not the same. I know this sounds corny, but I think it was because I didn't love him. I didn't think of Bobby until Josh was satisfied. Then it hit me like a ton of bricks. I had violated our love. There could never be the feelings of forever with Bobby again. I desecrated what was truly pure. The innocence we both brought to each other was so childlike, so virginal, and so special. Maybe first love is like that for most everyone. I don't know, but, nothing has had the same intensity. I have a strong feeling that nothing ever will. That thought leaves me with an empty depressed feeling."

Stephanie is a divorced thirty-nine-year-old mother of a six-year-old daughter. She is also an attorney, employed by a large metropolitan law firm, specializing in corporate law. Last year she went to her gynecologist after feeling a lump in her right breast. Within the week she had the lump surgically removed. Since she had no history of a cystic condition, her physician was concerned. He knew about the increased risk of breast and cervical cancer in divorced and widowed women. And he knew that having had her first full-term pregnancy after the age of thirty also placed Stephanie in a higher-risk category. So rather than take a wait-and-see attitude he preferred to be cautious. He had the lump biopsied, and it was reported to be benign.

A very rare occurrence followed. The microscope slide was labeled "benign fibro cystic breast disease" and sent to a local medical school. A third-year medical student, having taken a look at the slide, was puzzled by the similarity that the textbook picture of breast carcinoma had with the slide in his microscope. He called over the professor to tell him that the slide seemed to be improperly labeled. The elderly professor's face flushed as he told the student that he was correct. He pointed out to the student how the encapsulating cells appeared benign, but the more central one got, the more malignant the cells appeared to be. Actually he was talking out loud to himself as he tried to reconcile the mistake with the seriousness of the consequences.

The older man left the lab muttering that he had never, in almost thirty years of teaching, been witness to such negligence. Once in his office he called the pathology department at the hospital that prepared the slides. He said it was most urgent that he be informed of the name of the surgeon who provided the cyst from which the slide was prepared. His call was returned within the hour. The surgeon was totally cooperative. He said that he had never encountered such a happening either and that the pathologist would have some explaining to do.

Eventually the error was found to have been made by the pathologist. After making certain from other slides prepared from the same "cyst," Stephanie was told the bad news. She had been greatly relieved when the first report came back. Her feelings now raced from panic to denial and back to panic. Couldn't this second reading be a mistake instead of the first one?

The surgeon, trying to calm her, explained that in effect she had undergone a lumpectomy of a malignancy, which would have been his choice of treatment even if he had known the tumor was malignant before the operation. But when he stated that women who have mastectomies rather than lumpectomies do not seem to do any better over the years, Stephanie took this to mean that she was doomed. Her state of mind was not helped when he added that in his opinion this "tumor" had been growing for anywhere from two to four years. That put its origin back to the time when her husband began the affair that led to their divorce.

"Jim was never anything special. As a matter of fact, after Josh there were a lot of guys. Jim was similar to Josh, and he was on the scene when I was vulnerable. After getting caught up in the need to be an assertive, successful woman, I also got caught up in the need to abandon any restrictions on sexuality.

"But every time I thought of Bobby I first felt warm and, well,

26

soft again. Then these feelings turned to depression. Josh fell by the wayside. He was more interested in his appearance and how other women, I should say girls, perceived him. Any moron, other than this one, would have seen him as a womanizer. I always felt amazingly alone after having sex with him. Oh, he was good. He prided himself on making sure I was pleased. So much so that I felt I had to fake it at times or he would have been crushed. It was the same with my ex-husband . . .

"Well, anyway, after Josh there were about seven or eight other guys in college. In law school I even made it with two married professors, father figures, I guess. But then there were the other students. It seems that almost every time I studied with a male colleague I wound up in bed with him. Frankly, I began to get really depressed and feel a little, no, a lot, like a slut. I finally decided that it was my liberal sexual life-style that was depressing me.

"But regardless of knowing this, I still occasionally hopped into the sack. Every time I felt depressed afterward. I began to think I was never going to get married when I met Jim—tall, dark, and handsome Jim. He interviewed me for the job at the law firm. I immediately knew he was interested in me, and I also knew that I was going to get the job.

"Right after I started I made friends with one of the paralegals. She told me that Jim was dating someone else. I was actually shocked when he asked me out. Me, shocked. I slept with two married professors in law school, and I was shocked by a guy who was almost engaged asking me out. Maybe I was shocked that a guy that good-looking was asking me out. But why should I be? Josh and almost all the others were good-looking. I guess I am at least a little attractive. At least on the outside. The truth is I know I'm good-looking. I just don't like myself. I couldn't really relate to any of these men, to any men. I enjoyed them but still felt I could not really let go like I did with Bobby. I was always vaguely uncomfortable. Nothing was clear, but something was wrong.

"When Jim found Nancy I knew it before he told me. I was a wreck. It was strange because I already knew I did not love him. But the thought of losing him was intolerable. It was an indictment of my inadequacy. He did not matter. The truth, again? I don't think anyone has ever really mattered. Maybe my daughter, but I'm not sure even she matters to me. It's like I'm destined to have a horrible sense of aloneness. I'm sure this is connected to my cancer in some way. Oh, I know all about diet and not smoking, but I always paid attention to what the experts said not to eat. I never smoked. I rarely drink. I'm an exercise fanatic. And damn it, I got cancer! Why me? My carcinogen is unhappiness. I'm the essence of Yuppie. We all lead healthy, active lives. And we seem to be getting cancer after cancer. I'm certainly not the only person in my life-style with a history of cancer. It's getting to the point where it seems everyone will wind up with cancer. The newspaper said that one out of three Americans will get it, and that it's getting worse, not better.

"I know what caused my cancer. It wasn't bacon or cigarettes or red meat. It was loneliness, depression, and feeling unconnected. If I could have stayed loyal to Bobby, my life might have been totally different, and I know I would not have developed this rotten cancer. Maybe I should say 'rotting' cancer. I feel every ache and pain, every pimple is the breast cancer spreading. It's so horrible to have to be this scared. And if any of the men in my past had been a Bobby I wouldn't have gotten it. Having those negative painful feelings year after year, from my childhood on, has to have one hell of a negative effect on my body. When are those researchers going to wake up?

"My friends and I all agree that their 'discoveries' are meaningless in most of our lives. All of my friends who smoke can't stop just because the Cancer Society says to. My friends don't know if they should go for these, quote, low dosage, unquote, mammographies or not. I read that some doctors say those X rays will increase the risk of getting breast cancer. Then you should have chest X rays and drink that chalk and enema X rays? Come on, who's going to go through all that testing? You'd glow in the dark! And what if they find something anyway? The Cancer Society says you live longer and have a better chance if diagnosis is early. But I read that some experts say that is all a pack of lies. That like with me, for example, if twenty-five years ago they would have diagnosed my breast cancer it would have been there from four to six years before they could tell. They also told me the average life span for breast cancer is still about seven years. So now they diagnosed me after maybe two years. So someone twenty-five years ago would have only a year or two to live after the diagnosis, and I can figure on four or five years.

"They claim they increased longevity one hundred percent. They lie all the time. All they've done is diagnose earlier. I keep reading about this, and I am convinced we're being lied to. Eat fiber and avoid cancer. Do this or don't do that, and you won't get cancer. I wish it was really that simple. Why do they keep ignoring what almost everyone knows—that cancer is tied to your life-style, your ability to relate, and how miserable you are when you don't or can't relate.

"All those corny values of days of yore are suddenly making more and more sense to me. Weren't the cancer rates lower when people really condemned adultery and divorce? Weren't they lower when families mattered and stayed together?

"I know, it's a virus, right? Well, why haven't they found it? With AIDS they found the virus in what, two or three years? If there was a virus for breast or colon or lung cancer, don't you think they would have found it by now?

"Wasn't it in the early seventies that Nixon declared war on cancer? He said, and the experts said, we'd have it beaten within ten years. I'm waiting, Mr. Nixon and your experts. But I may not have that much time to wait.

"Why can't they see that it's how we lead our lives, not just the simplistic 'whats' that make up our lives that is the answer? I'm a

29

lawyer, a mother, a rejected, husbandless woman. I'm not a doctor. What can I know? I'll tell you, I can know a lot more than the microscopic voyeurs in the laboratories. I have had years in my laboratory brewing up that lump in my breast. The laboratory is me and my life history. I know, that's right, *know* that my lump is from my inability to accept love and caring from others. It's from my confusion over what sex is all about. It's from the beginning of my life up to the present. This is the way I have always been. I can't stay this way and beat my cancer. I must change. But I know I can't do it alone. Being a macho-Yuppie woman is going to kill me.

"There's more to life than money and status. There's more to life than being strong all the time. There's more to life than sex for sex's sake. There's more to life than just me!"

Stephanie is right. She is a remarkable, intuitive woman whose very unscientific feelings are right on target. We are first beginning to demonstrate "scientifically" what Stephanie already knows. We "know" that divorced or widowed women in America and Great Britain have a significantly higher breast and cervical cancer rate than married women. We know that men who are Type A personalities between the ages of twenty-five and forty are more likely to have prostatitis. After the age of forty, men who have intermittent or inadequate sexual contacts are much more likely to develop prostate cancer. There is no nutritional, carcinogen, viral, or hereditary explanation to explain prostate cancer.

On the questionnaires that most of us have received in the mail from such organizations as the American Cancer Society, we are asked whether we are single, married, divorced, or widowed. The questionnaires do not ask about the quality of our marriages. Is the wife an alcoholic? Has the husband been adulterous? Do you love your spouse? Are you sexually satisfied? Do you think your spouse is? How often does he claim he's too tired? How many headaches does she have per week?

If divorced was the box you checked, the questionnaire should ask whether the marriage ended amicably. Were both parties happy to unload the other? Was there a fear of future relationships? Is sport sex the new recreation?

In widowhood the questions that are relevant are also not being asked. How would the marriage be characterized? What was the cause of death? How was grief dealt with? Did adult children support and console? Was the survivor encouraged to seek social contact?

Dr. R. W. Bartrop of Australia and Dr. Steven Schleifer of New York found out in their laboratories that certain white cells (the ones that help consume bacteria and other foreign bodies) are suppressed during grief reactions. When these T-lymphocytes are not produced, obviously the person is less able to fend off infections and destroy evolving cancer cells. Everyone knows of cases in which one member of a happy marriage dies and the other develops a malignancy within a year or two. Loss correlates with cancer. Stephanie knows this.

Dr. David Garrabrant at U.S.C. did a study that demonstrated that longshoremen have the lowest rate of colorectal tumors in America. He found that among occupations, computer programmers have the highest incidence. Are we to believe that longshoremen pay more attention to nutrition than computer programmers? A cheeseburger with pickles, a beer, and probably a cigarette are not an unusual lunch for these people who blow off steam all day long through physical work. Computer programmers are far more likely to be eating carrot sticks and whole wheat bread. The longshoremen don't get colorectal tumors and the computer programmers do. Perhaps, it's not what we eat, but how we eat that is the issue.

The sad fact seems to be that promises from the "responsible" segments of cancer research have not been kept. We have seen the failure of interferon. We are being told by respected medical researchers (Dr. Michael B. Shimkim, Professor Emeritus, Uni-

31

versity of California, San Diego) that chemotherapies are more than questionable in many instances. We are waiting for mono-colonal antibodies and are being told progress is being made inch by inch. That is simply not good enough for those already suffering from a cancer.

We are all beginning to question medical concepts and dogma. There are too many unanswered questions. The scientific approach is not succeeding in some areas. Respected practitioners and scientists are raising the issues themselves.

The American medical community is a remarkably valued and respected part of our society. Nowhere else in the world are doctors so revered. But when it comes to chronic degenerative disorders such as cancer or cardiovascular or neurological problems, for far too many cases the profession fails miserably. Anyone who credits increased longevity to modern medicine is, at the least, a bit naive. First of all, from the age of forty-five until death, longevity has not increased significantly in the last twenty-five years. In the decade of 1960-70, the average life span actually decreased.

Americans pay the highest per capita medical costs in the world, and we rate thirty-third for men and twenty-first for women in life span. We are fifteenth in infant mortality. Sweden, which uses midwives instead of obstetricians to deliver babies, has a lower maternal and infant mortality rate. We turn pregnancy and childbirth into a disease.

Where modern medicine does extremely well is in the treatment of trauma (auto accidents and other similar type injuries) and acute infections. Antibiotics have been a godsend. But outside these two categories, the medical profession is making little or no headway.

The doctor's oath to not make matters worse for a patient has all too often been ignored by the overzealous physician attempting to avoid feeling impotent in the treatment of cancer. Standard medical techniques for cancer amount to cutting, burning, or poisoning. When these approaches are applied to people with little or no chance of them being effective, we can see that the respected medical establishment is practicing quackery. Certain of these techniques seem to be effective for very limited types of cancer. Discomfort and side effects should be tolerated in such instances. But to torture people with almost no medical chance is absurd. These people need to be kept comfortable. The issue of quality of life is important.

Bear in mind that no one gets better who stops eating, moving, or relating to other people. Any doctor who condemns a patient to bed is condemning him to death. The side effects of cancer seem to progress much more rapidly in people not eating or moving.

If our medical gods cannot help effectively to prevent and reverse cancers, who can? It is up to all of us to reduce the incidence of cancer in our society. Not by donating time or money to further microscopic myopia, but through the recognition that life-style is the key.

Before we even had a test for tuberculosis, the incidence of the disease was greatly reduced. Medicine was not the cause of this drastic reduction. Nutrition, sanitation, and working conditions all improved, and TB was reduced. New disorders to replace it have evolved. The disorder of our times is cancer.

The other epidemic in our midst is not frequently considered when disease or disorders are discussed. But depression is rampant in American, Swedish, and Japanese societies. Cancer is also epidemic. The two are definitely, in my opinion, tied together. We must appreciate at least the possibility of their inconspicuous connection. Depression does lead to alcohol and cigarette usage. It is certainly tied in to overeating. It thus predisposes an individual to exposure to powerful carcinogens. At the same time it frequently is characterized by lethargy and under use of the musculature. Almost everyone is depressed at times. But when it is habitual, it connects to cancers.

We can see that in each era new diseases, like herpes and AIDS, evolve. Frequently they almost vanish, not because of what modern medicine accomplishes, but because of what all of us accomplish. We change our life-styles. Cancer is a direct outcome of negative life-styles. Maybe we can learn to eat less and better foods. Maybe we can reduce harshness in our environments as much as possible. And maybe we can see that in every area of the world where the extended family exists the cancer rate and depression statistics are lower. In America, Sweden, and gradually even in Japan the family is dissolving and cancer rates are rising. The basis of the integrity of any family is the relationship between the parents, the marriage. Successful, properly balanced, loving marriage is life sustaining. Divorce, widowhood, and, almost certainly, adultery is life threatening. Stephanie knows this. Statistics show this.

The truth, absolute, no-lie statistical truth, is that married people outlive single people by a significant margin. Why is this true in almost all societies? Marriage provides for a sharing of worries, depression, and anxieties. These feelings on a chronic level are biochemically destructive to our bodies. They stimulate production of adrenaline-based reactions. They keep us ready for flight or fight internally while our adult, mature minds tell us we cannot fight or flee. (As we are immobilized we stew in our own juices.)

Loving marriage throughout history has been the most effective means we have to lessen the impact of worry and fear. Just compare the differences in feeling that most people would experience in this extreme example: A soldier is sent out alone in enemy territory with a radio to reconnoitre an area believed to be a staging point for a massive attack. Fear of annihilation, fear of humiliation, fear of failure may plague this one poor soul to the extent that enough adrenaline is produced to last for years. He must fend for himself. He must get back by himself. If wounded, he must care for himself. He knows all this in advance of the mission.

Now, picture being a soldier in a regiment facing an enemy force. Certainly the fear of annihilation, humiliation, etc., will be operating. But it can be shared. You have learned to rely on your buddy to assist you. Certainly battle is terrifying. But facing it alone is the most terrifying experience any of us can endure. For most of us, our battles are waged on jobs, in offices, within professions, or in the strains of childrearing and household economics. They are less intense, but they are usually far more habitual and prolonged. Stephanie's loneliness is one such chronic battle. Facing her disorder alone will be certain doom. She knows this. She prefers, or claims to prefer, having a buddy to help face her battles. Being a recon commando is not very appealing in the face of cancer.

Throughtout the remaining chapters I will discuss the underlying dynamics of courtship and marriage. We will see how love and acceptance can help create a healthy, biochemical, internal environment for both partners. Most important, I will point out practical steps we can all take to change patterns that add to internal pollution in ourselves and our spouses. We will compare the carcinogenic marriage to the anti-cancer marriage.

The need for candor about loving feelings and sexuality will be appreciated. You will see that I believe the two cannot be separated. Romance and sex have always gone together. When interviews are quoted, sex will be dealt with as candidly as the interviewees did. It is amazing how candid people can be if they know it is for a good reason.

By the way, Stephanie is a real person. She is also very much alive and showing no signs of active cancer. Her medical treatment included chemotherapy. But she is convinced that her good health is based upon her new marriage. He is two years younger than she. He is not an Adonis. He is not even a lawyer. But he loves her, and she is learning to accept it and love back. He knows her history of malignancy and helps her face it. They share it. She's going to make it!

2

Courtship

FREUD WAS A BRILLIANT, creative man and an innovative, courageous pioneer in the realm of the psyche, but he was wrong. And he was the first to say that his ideas would eventually be proven wrong and would be revised as more and more evidence was compiled. He did not see his thought processes as a religion. It is a pity that his disciples did and still do.

In the terms of courtship he produced a theory commonly referred to as the Oedipal Complex (Electra for females). Basically, he suggested that boys between the ages of three and seven years begin to grow into real men by emulating their fathers and sexually desiring mom. In a rather chauvinistic view of women, he saw them doing the reverse, of course, with the addition of overwhelmingly envying the potency in sex, and life in general, that the phallus represented. His mistake was in not appreciating the need we all have to reexperience the feelings of pleasurable fusion or bonding we had in early infancy. He also believed that the experiences of this earliest stage could not be later dealt with psychoanalytically.

Dr. Freud, the truth seems to be that both men and women marry their earliest maternal figures. If we are able to expose our frailties and make ourselves vulnerable to our spouses, it is indicative of the predominantly loving care we received as newborns. At weddings we speak of the need to have and to hold, in sickness and in health, for better or worse. New mothers could make the same vows to their newborns, and it would be totally appropriate.

However, not everyone grows up to be open and warm and able to fuse with others just as no mother can be perfect, and no woman should assume that it is even a remote possibility. The baby stays within us all, revealing him- or herself through symptoms of the nervous system, whether anxiety, depression, psychosomatic problems, or a fear of relating.

No marriage can be perfect, and it is absurd for us to assume such a state is within reach. But as adults we can do something about the inadequacies in our lives—our marriages in particular. If we do, it is more than likely we can help influence the mental and physical health of ourselves and spouses. At the least we can improve the quality of our emotional and sexual lives.

In 1950, 80 percent of American women getting married were virgins. In 1980 we achieved the numerical reversal: 20 percent of the women were virgins until marriage. The obvious and very important question seems to be: Does this in any way relate to divorce and/or higher incidence of cancer?

In the thirty years referred to, we were witness to the "sexual revolution." The gurus of unchecked libidinal expression of the sixties and seventies promised sexual fulfillment, lowered levels of "uptightness," and far greater happiness in general. What has happened has been an increase in new and more deadly venereal diseases. What has happened is an increase in feelings of sexual inadequacy and dysfunctions. What has happened is a general epidemic of depression (and cancer), which is frequently related to inadequate sexuality and an inability to be in a fusional life-sustaining relationship.

The gurus of the sexual revolution knew very little of actual human dynamics. They did not know that increased sexual freedom would translate to confusion of life-style roles, gender identity problems, and a need for an entire new psycho-medical field to deal with sexual inadequacies. The Abie Hoffmans and Timothy Learys did little to reduce anxiety and suffering in a conflictual world.

Our teachers must do research into what our elders knew. We must learn from what worked for them and what did not. When we encounter people who have been happily married for fifty or more years, we must recognize that we have a mother lode of vital information to help us understand successful marriage and, perhaps, longevity itself.

WALTER AND HANNAH are in their mid-eighties. They have been happily married for sixty-eight years. They have lived on Long Island all their lives. Three of their five children are alive, married, and successful. They have eight grandchildren and four great-grandchildren. Their home is a lovely Victorian house near the ocean. Furnishings are old and comfortable. You can stop to appreciate a couch or table and sense the warmth that made up their family. Photos in porcelain frames are everywhere. Hannah has a delightful collection of music boxes in a corner cabinet with scroll carvings and inlays of different woods. Most of them were gifts from Walter. They appear very valuable, but to Hannah, they are priceless.

"We got married just before I joined the Marines to stop the Huns. Huns, ha! We should have sowed their soil with salt before that lunatic Hitler came to power. Hannah was sixteen, and I was just eighteen. She was a real heartthrob. Here I was, this tough, rough, young Marine going off to war, and this girl with the long blond hair turned me into mush."

"Oh, Walter, you still carry on with that talk! Young man, my Walter was every girl's dream. He was a star athlete in high school, but he was smart too. When he told me he joined the

Marines, I almost fainted, but I knew somehow that he would come back to me."

"I'm glad you did because I had some times that I was quite sure I'd never see you again. At least on earth. When I got wounded it was such a relief to be knowing that I'd be home soon. I still limp from it, but I would have given my whole leg for five minutes with her. I lost so many dear friends. They were just boys who had not even begun life yet. I guess it was the same for the Kaiser's troops."

Walter's eyes began to fill up at this point. His hair is pure white and his eyes are steel gray. The first thing that strikes you about him is his posture. He still carries himself like an eighteen-year-old Marine. He is not tense, he is just very upright for a man of eighty-six. The lines in his face are subtle and gentle, particularly when he smiles. His eyes still twinkle. He is a big man who somehow exudes an impishness when he talks. One can easily see the powerful young Marine who once lived in those muscles and skin.

"Walter almost died of grief when our Matthew was killed in World War II. He was such a darling boy. They gave me a medal and a flag in a ceremony. I don't think either one of us could have survived when Sarah took sick and died three years later, if we didn't have one another and all our family and friends. They never did know for sure but years later, Dr. Stan told us it probably was some infection of the heart. She was so close to Matthew."

"Hannah," Walter interrupted, "this young doctor is not here to talk to us about our losses and grief. Stop doing this to yourself. It's over forty years now." He put his hand on her shoulder.

Hannah looked up, first at Walter and then at me. Her eyes were a deep blue. Her skin was wrinkled, but amazingly soft looking. She was a slender, petite woman who wore her still-long hair up in a bun. Hannah looks like what an old "lady" is supposed ideally to look like. She has a grace and easiness about her.

Most of all, she is still in love. She coughed a little to clear her throat.

"I am an only child. My daddy was a doctor, and I was the apple of his eye. My mother, let me show you . . . [She got up and brought over an old photo of a magnificently beautiful woman and a husky young man with a baby on his lap.] That's me and my folks when I was two. I think this was taken in Chicago. Daddy went to school there. Mother was Scottish, just off the boat. And Daddy was half-English and half-Swedish. His parents had lived here all their lives. I think they were always in love, but they had plenty left for me. Mostly, I remember what she smelled like—fresh and clean, with the slightest hint of perfume. You can't see it in the picture, but she had beautiful long, red hair with the greenest eyes. He was short and stocky, a powerful man, but so gentle. He had hands like a woman. I don't really remember, but I was told that a maternal aunt lived with us until I was two and a half. She got married and moved. I had lots of aunts and uncles and cousins to play with from my father's side. It was so different then. Violence and sex were equally obscene to most people, not like today. Oh, kids played doctor and had crushes on each other, but there was romance. The world is so cold without romance. Walter was so romantic. I was fifteen when I first saw him. We were never allowed to be alone together though."

"It drove me crazy. Here was this beautiful girl and all we could do was hold hands. I knew something was up, every time I was with her I got embarrassed and was confused. I knew what the horses did, but the feelings were confusing."

"Walter, shut up!"

"Hannah, this is not a Friday night poker game. I'm only telling him all this for science. He is doing research on what keeps people going, right? Hannah and I both loved making love and never refused each other. But if one was sick or exhausted, we knew not to make any demands. We always slept close to each other. But I'm jumping the gun. After a while we got to be alone."

"That's right. We lied to do it, but we had to. The truth is, I was all over him. We didn't even know what we were doing, but we did it anyway. I mean smooching. Not . . . you know."

"I used to love to bring her small things, gifts. I'd put flowers in her hair in the springtime. That first summer together was rough on the beach! Swimsuits were hot. So we spent most of the time in the water. She grabbed me first and the rest of the summer we were waterlogged. We figured no one could tell, but now I realize everyone probably knew.

"I think they did. At least Sissy knew—that's my older sister. She teased me. She was four years older and helped raise me. I was the second born, and it was pretty strange in those days not to have kids one after another. After me my two brothers came along. I've outlived all of them." He stopped and smilingly offered me a cigarette. "This is how I met this scientist, dear. We were on line at the bank. He was right in front of me, when he smelled my cigarette. He turned around and very politely asked my permission to ask me a question. You don't run into young people that polite too often anymore. Anyway he wanted to know how many packs of cigarettes I smoke. I told him I cut back to one and a half. He asked me how long I've been smoking. I told him ever since I married you and that you still hated it. The truth is I did start smoking almost seventy years ago. But I started in his lord Woodrow Wilson's own Royal Marines. We got them for free so even though I'm not Scottish, I couldn't see giving them away. Maybe I was a little nervous, and it became a habit." He looked at Hannah. "Okay, no more Scottish jokes. She used to get really peeved when I teased her."

"And you always talked like you're from New York City. No class, no class. Anyway, tell him of your family. He wants to know."

"My parents were wealthy. My father made money in the lumber business. Rich private housing was going up even on Long Island after the first war. Long Island was terrific in those days. You could hunt or fish all over the place. The water was so clean in the three rivers out there no one thought twice about drinking from it. I'd like to go quail hunting where I used to, but there are so many split levels, if I fired my Browning Five even once, I'd get arrested for mass murder. Ha . . . Hannah never liked hunting, but she could really drift a dry fly. And did those trout taste good fresh from the stream. Should I tell him?"

"Oh, go ahead."

"We snuck away one time while fishing on the Carmen's River. We had the canoe, some sandwiches, and soda pop. Everybody else stayed in the lake, and we paddled up the river a piece. When we realized we were really alone, we did it for the first time."

"What he is saying is made love. And it was beautiful. We haven't stopped since. But we both knew that meant we were going to get married and soon."

"I asked her father's permission the next day. I was upset that it happened before we were married. And before there was a chance of her being pregnant, I wanted to marry her. I was leaving for the Corps in three and a half weeks. We would have anyway but, boy, was I shocked when he said yes. Our parents were friends, and I think they all knew it was coming. But she was just sixteen, and I figured they'd want us to wait. Thank God they didn't."

"His folks tried to get me to maybe wait until he got back. I think, God forbid, they were worried I might be left a very young widow. I told him that I was a woman and wanted to spend every minute I could with him before, during, and after the war. His mom winked at me, and to this day I think she knew what I really caught up on the Carmen's River. We were married four days later."

"Yes, we spent our honeymoon in the Waldorf Astoria in New York. Actually, we barely got out to see the city. Time flies when you're having fun and before we knew it, I was on a train to boot camp. I was away from her for two weeks when I thought I'd go crazy. The chaplain helped. My war was over eleven months later. During that time we wrote some steamy letters to each other. It started off almost like friends writing, but then got more and more romantic and, well, sexy. We still have every letter. They must be almost seventy years old. Maybe I could sell them as valuable historical documents."

After World War I, Walter worked in the family business, eventually taking over ownership. Hannah raised children and later became a registered nurse.

They are a delightful couple. Listening to them over a period of time made it clear that their love started off special and has remained so over sixty-eight years. They obviously still really enjoy each other. I couldn't help but feel uplifted after the first five minutes of our interview. Like depression, happiness is contagious. But what else makes these two and their love so special? 1) They and their era made sex romantic, private, and special. 2) They were able to share the ultimate grief of having lost children. At the time, the biochemical irritants of grief were dissipated in each other, through their fusion. 3) They are fun people with an appreciation for each other's sense of humor. 4) They respect each other's feelings.

This all started in their courtship. We can surmise that like most first-love situations they became obsessed with each other. The obsession and passion duplicated the passion of the positive mother-infant bond. This fusion is what is life sustaining to the infant's biology and nervous system. It is what is life sustaining to children and adults as well. People who reverse cancers seem always to have some relationship that replicates this bond. This bond, which Hannah and Walter developed in courtship, is present in every case I have studied of spontaneous cure of cancer (people getting better with little or no medical treatment). They did not fear to be totally dependent upon each other at critical points in their lives. If either Walter or Hannah or both had had a basically negative very early infantile experience, they would have been afraid of such a fusion.

Their times had vigorous restrictions on sexuality. According to Freud, this supposedly was the cause of all sorts of symptoms, but many mental health professionals today see bottled-up anger and rage as far more symptom related. I'm not advocating as extreme a degree of sexual restriction as existed at the beginning of the century, but if a society is too casual about sex, it is almost impossible for the individual to keep it in proper perspective. If a society is too casual about sex, it appears to be too casual about love. If a society loses its need for romance, the maternal-infant bond will not be replicated in adulthood. Recent research indicates that lack of such relationships is tied into many different mind-related physical disorders: cancer, cardiovascular disorders, and perhaps even certain neurological disorders.

Hannah and Walter are unique in many ways. They have already well surpassed the average American life expectancy. They have been married almost as long as the average American survives. But what is most unique about them is the playfulness and sexual balance that started in their courtship and continues to the present. When this balance is not present, angry or rejected feelings are a dominant feature of a relationship. When sexual desire is inequitable both sides suffer. Usually the underlying causes relate to the need for distance and pushing away learned in infancy.

CHARLIE IS A kind, considerate, sexually inhibited man. Over the seventeen years that he has been married, his wife has frequently considered leaving him. She holds out by rationalizing that he is the sweetest man she has ever known. He provides adequately for her and their two daughters.

Charlie is most comfortable and secure at home, exactly there, at home. He plays catcher on a slow pitch softball team. Saturday morning league games get Charlie through the week. The wives almost all used to go to the games and make a picnic out of the after-game celebration or solace, but gradually, fewer and fewer of the wives continued to attend. The laughter of the players' children gradually was replaced by the macho catcalls ball players frequently exchange. Eventually, what started out as a family Saturday morning ritual turned into the likes of a beer commercial.

Charlie used his early morning wake-up as an excuse for getting to sleep early on Friday nights with no lovemaking. Saturday night, the excuse was his soreness or exhaustion from the game. But there always seems to be an excuse. When sex does infrequently occur, it is his wife who initiates it. She is willing to do almost anything to please him, but he is close to being phobic when it comes to the female body.

"When I was a kid my friends all dated before I did. They would try to fix me up, and every time I fought. But if I did go out I had fun. But no matter how many times my friends set me up, I always anticipated making a jerk out of myself. In the locker room the boys would talk about what they were doing with different girls. Oh, some others didn't brag about that stuff either. I felt it was really dirty pool to get a girl involved and then talk behind her back. The boys were pretty graphic at times, and I have to admit I got embarrassed. They'd say things like, Hey guys I grabbed Margie's boobs this weekend. They're huge and stick out like 105 artillery shells. That's it, Margie has 105's. That was sort of okay, but if they spoke of what actually happened sexually I got really upset. My friend Steve was dating a girl named Monica. One time Steve gave a detailed explanation of Monica performing on him. The others were spellbound, but I felt humiliated. I tried to hide it, but I'm not sure I did. They told me I was a pussy and would probably be unable to get it up if a girl did that to me." The strange part is they were right. It took a long time for me to trust my wife enough to enjoy that.

"I met Sue Ellen when I was in the Navy. I was born in West Virginia and joined the Navy right after high school. You know to see the world and all. I was a corpsman on a cruiser off the coast of Vietnam for six months. Thank God I wasn't assigned to a land-based unit. Anyway, I was on liberty in Hawaii when I met her. She was very attractive and very shy. She seemed to sense my shyness, and we immediately hit it off. She was from Ohio and was attending the University of Hawaii. I told her that I only had two weeks, and we'd be going back. It turned out that I was reassigned to a hospital near Pearl. I did a whole tour there, and our relationship grew. She asked me out after we met. She said it was the least she could do for a serviceman. We went to the Hilton for dinner and a floor show. That's when I figured her folks had money. She told me she wasn't working but wouldn't let me pay for anything. She dropped me off at the base, and we parked for a couple of minutes and talked. As we talked, I looked at her chest and got an erection. She moved closer and kissed me, and instantly I lost it. That freaked me out. But I, of course, didn't let her know. We made a date for the next night. I told her that I had lots of money from being at sea for all that time. We ate at the most expensive restaurant I could find. I think I was the only enlisted man there. Lots of officers and I felt uncomfortable. Sue Ellen sensed this on the dance floor and suggested we leave and walk for a while. Instead we drove up on Pali Highway, I think to a place called Kunia. We parked and started to make out. Yeah, she started it again, come to think of it. It felt good, but again no erection. I could not get an erection with her whenever we were close. I could do it several times a day by myself. I fantasized about someone just like Sue Ellen, but when I finally had an actual Sue Ellen, I couldn't even get it up.

"Things progressed, and the kissing got more passionate. I was falling in love, and so was she. We were on the beach at night. I was in my whites, and she had on bermuda shorts and a blouse. She unbuttoned it and put my hand on her breast. It felt so good and so weird. Her hands were under my uniform. She touched me, and I was able to keep my erection, thank goodness. I touched her, and she showed me how. She had an orgasm. It seemed all sort of ridiculous to me, but I stayed excited. She tried to get me off with her hand, but no dice. I kept my hard-on, but I thought her arm would fall off. She switched hands and finally gave up. Sue was so sweet. She told me not to worry. That she had all the time in the world and that she knew it would be all right. I lied to her and told her this never happened before and that it was because I never loved a girl before, that the feelings were overwhelming. She told me that she loved me and always would.

"Do you know what? We did not have sex for six weeks. Again, I was forced to see that I had a major problem. I just feel weird when I'm that close to her. It's damned uncomfortable. If I'm turned on enough I can enjoy it. But I always need to jump out of bed and go to the bathroom. She says she wants to cuddle. I just feel suffocated and need to wash. For a while I thought she'd leave me. Maybe, as she said, that's what I wanted. It's hard to believe that, though, because I really think I love her. I'm a nice guy. I'm a giving person. I was when we were dating. For some reason I'm just not a very sexual person."

Charlie shows signs of obvious sexual inhibitions now as he did during courtship. The symptoms can be treated by sex therapists. However, the underlying causes of such a fear of being close are the really destructive elements to be addressed. Orgasm in the presence of another person is frightening to Charlie. Alone, he is quite capable of reaching orgasm. Then what does orgasm or sex in general mean to him? Perhaps this closeness represents a real return to a powerful negative relationship he had in infancy. If Charlie's first relationship in life was fraught with anxiety and fear of being overwhelmed by an intermittently irritated mother, then he would have been programmed to expect some danger in intimate closeness. Regardless of how loving and giving Sue Ellen was, or is, she still represents someone to be feared. Charlie is transferring his early feelings toward his mother onto Sue Ellen. Reasoning and rationality have nothing to do with it: The involuntary nervous system was conditioned that way. Every time Charlie's erection fades, every time he has to jump right out of bed, every time he tries to avoid the epitome of what makes up the female anatomy, involuntary aspects of the nervous system cause adrenaline-based reactions to flow because of his need to fight or, more appropriately, flee. Nothing in Charlie's conscious mind is telling him danger is present, but what Charlie describes as a "weird" feeling is his entire physiology reacting as if there were real danger. The bodily reactions will win out until Charlie's involuntary nervous system can be reeducated. Sue Ellen is not in the position to provide the corrective experience. She has been too angry and has felt rejected for far too long. They both know that.

Charlie entered analytic treatment several months ago. The therapist received a thank-you note from Sue Ellen recently. Had Charlie not begun to resolve his problems in treatment, it is very likely that one or both could have developed a serious psychosomatic disorder. There is very good reason for optimism about these two.

PAULA IS CASUAL about sex. In 1982, Paula was diagnosed as suffering from a diffuse, non-Hodgkins, malignant lymphoma. She was immediately placed on chemotherapy. Her white blood cell count stayed at a range of 2,500 to 2,700 for three years. Low normal for a woman is 4,000. In 1984, Paula entered a new type of psychotherapy designed to reeducate the nervous system in ways that lower adrenaline-based reactions and raise neuroimmunological functions (see my previous book, *The Causes and Prevention of Cancer*). She has been encouraged to stick with her chemotherapy in spite of the fact that her oncologist told her she had only a .001 percent chance of surviving her lymphoma. Since she began psychotherapy her white blood cell count has remained predominantly stable at between 6,700 and 7,000. When she is depressed and fighting treatment it will fall to 5,000, still very much within a normal healthy range. On four separate occasions her cancer specialists have tried to do biopsies (punch biopsies) but could find nothing to biopsy. Granted lymphomas have ups and downs characteristically, but Paula's lymphoma improved immediately upon entering treatment and has remained so. Perhaps it is coincidence, or perhaps her psychotherapy is responsible. Several years from now we can be more certain. In the meantime she is doing better than well with an unexpected white cell count even in the face of chemotherapy. Her oncologist admits to being perplexed.

"My courtship with Jeff? Courtship, God, I haven't heard that word in years. Nobody even uses it anymore. You're so quaint. Before Jeff there were other men. Please don't be shocked, but as a matter of fact, one of my favorite regular dates was with the Seventh Fleet. Let's say I was not exactly a puritan.

"You think all of that stuff has to do with my cancer. Okay, I'll talk. But it does depress me when I even think of it."

Paula has three young sons. Up until her cancer she left them in the care of a nanny-housekeeper. She worked as a copywriter in a large Manhattan advertising firm. Just before she became pregnant with her first boy she was promoted. She took only six weeks off when the baby was born. She did the same with the others. And she continued to move up the ladder. Money was not the issue: Her husband, Jeff, is a very successful accountant with his own company. Paula simply has a need to be doing and achieving.

She is an exceptionally attractive woman with short, stylish black hair and blue eyes. Her figure is excellent and reflects her frequent visits to her new religious shrine—her gym. She is there every day of the week for at least an hour.

"Well, let's see, before I met Jeff there really were far too many other men. I was twenty-eight when I got married and figured time was just beginning to run out on my biological clock to have babies. Let's see . . . I was fourteen when I first touched a boy. Mom always made a point of telling me nothing about sex. Let's just say it was embarrassing when as soon as I touched this cute

50

kid he orgasmed all over my hand. I mean I didn't know what happened, or if I should be embarrassed for him or not. Well, I'll admit it, I thought he had peed. After I regained my composure I started a lifelong love affair with the male organ. I could see why some cultures worship them. The trouble in hindsight was that I didn't care too much who they were attached to. I mean I thought I was in love with all of those nice boys at first, but then I realized that it was sex that intrigued me. They were toys to me, not people.

"My erogenous zones were sufficiently educated for graduate studies when I went off to college. When any of these boys tried to give me things like little cutesy stuffed animals or other gifts, that ended the relationship. I was really falling for one guy when I was nineteen. He gave me a dozen long-stemmed roses for my birthday. I broke up with him a week later. I just could not put up with that stuff. Even today if old stick in the mud, you know, Jeff, gets me jewelry or perfume, I am very uncomfortable. My friends have no trouble taking what they can get.

"Let's see . . . Okay, I went off to college. You know—drugs, drugs, drugs, followed by sex, sex, sex. Then we got creative and it was drugs, sex, drugs, sex. I look at pictures of myself from then, and I was a knockout. But I always looked smilingly sad. I spoke to a lot of people when I was hospitalized. I'm outgoing and friendly. Well so were a lot of the other people with cancers. You know, they were the president of the P.T.A. or the women's auxiliary or whatever. I always thought cancer people had no friends or at least were somewhat reclusive. You know what we are, we're a bunch of extroverts who don't really relate."

Analyst: "The lonely extroverts."

"Hey, Doc, do you want a job writing ads for gasoline or disposable diapers? See, I'd hire you and offer you the world so I could control you. Maybe I offered my body to men as a means of control. I did frequently get them to jump through hoops. I'm embarrassed to think I enjoyed being sadistic like that. But it was my way of controlling them. If I was the best they ever had they'd be my lambs. So disgusting but it works.

"Now Jeffrey was another story. We were fixed up by his sister. She and I were roommates. It was my senior year, and I was bored with the studs on campus. The porn movies and VCR's showed up at every fraternity party along with beer and drugs. I got bored very quickly watching that stuff. I still get bored by it. You know, insert tab A into slot B, reinsert, if necessary. What I used to do was watch everyone else watching the porn flicks. Let me tell you there is a big difference between men and women, at least most women. The men always get mesmerized, and the women always tried to seem cool, like it wasn't causing any reaction. Some of them looked like they were choking back barfing. Others were embarrassed to be turned on. Sex is different for men and women. Women need feeling more than men. Maybe we're just made to feel trampy if we do it just for fun. By now it wasn't fun anymore. I enjoyed it still, but it was boring.

"I told you I'd turn Hercules into a wimp. But Jeffrey just did not wimp out. He seemed to care less about me and my gorgeous body than I did about him. Somehow that lack of being swept off his feet fascinated and attracted me. Little did I know at that time that fifty megatons couldn't have swept him off his feet. It was a power play for him. He was just out to lunch a great deal of the time. I was the one who talked him into marriage. I talked him into having kids. If he'd have asked I think I really might have given up my career. The strangest part was that I even had to be the one who initiated sex all the time. To be honest, I never really enjoyed it with him. But to be really honest, I stopped being turned on some time in college. Oh, the first time it was always exciting. By the third or fourth time I was bored. It began to seem silly. By the time poor Jeffrey was on the scene, it didn't matter too much. What I didn't see was that it did not matter to him either. Do you know, I actually started buying him things? I never did that before. The whole thing was weird.

"As I put on my wedding gown, I felt like tingles all over. Then I was in a cold sweat. I jumped out of it, ran to the bathroom, and threw up. It took me a half hour to calm down. When I did I was numb. I thought I had a virus. I stayed sick one way or another until I got my cancer. I was sick a lot on chemo. But since I'm in treatment with you, come to think of it, I haven't felt sick.

"Well, Jeffrey is a hundred percent better too since he went into treatment. We actually talk now. And he's gotten to be a lot better in bed. I think maybe we are finally really falling in love. It's not part of courtship, but you know we did both have affairs before my lymphoma started up. He messed with some woman whose husband died and left her a fortune. I knew it so I retaliated with a guy at work who constantly was singing the 'my wife does not understand me' blues. But I realize it was out of anger and hurt that I did it. Yeah, I guess I did feel hurt by his affair. And for the first time I think I felt sexually inadequate. I stopped and he continued. I got cancer and he finally stopped. I went into this treatment and, knock wood, got better. He went into treatment and got sexier and even a little loving. I think we can really make it now. The amazing thing is that all the guys in my past were with it, together, and devoted to winning my little heart. So I wind up marrying a guy who is a world-class nerd. He really is a lot better now, but that's what I don't understand."

PROMISCUITY IS AN antiquated term. By today's standard perhaps it is no longer applicable. Sex, devoid of romance, is so common-place that we have all become somewhat desensitized as a society. Superficially, promiscuity may be viewed as just hyperactive sexual activity involving more than one partner. Beneath the surface it is a far more serious symptom of negative early learn-ing. Almost across the board in exploring such matters with patients and others, an inadequacy of the parenting experience is found. The promiscuous male or female is a prisoner of a need to repeat an aberrant mother-infant bond. And the repetition of a negative early infantile experience is a potential indicator of future psychosomatic disorders, cancer included. When the norms are in favor of promiscuity, the individual's ability to hold out for a "meaningful relationship" is depleted. After the first emotionally meaningless sexual experience, it is almost certainly easier for the next to occur.

The sexually inhibited avoid sex out of fear. The promiscuous engage in it out of fear. In both cases relating is permitted only up to a point, but when real loving feelings should evolve, both will desperately seek a distancing mechanism. In the deeply inhibited, any eroticism in the courtship will result in a need to flee. In the promiscuous, any re-experiencing of maternal-infant fusion, that sense of blending together, will result in a panic also marked by a need to flee. But the promiscuous, unlike the inhibited, will flee to the next sexual partner as a means of avoiding the intense bonding feelings of infancy. If that bond was even intermittently negative, it may be feared for a lifetime. If it was largely negative, that lifetime will not be a very happy or long one.

Every long-lived person I have interviewed—some over ninety, some even over a hundred years old—had memories of powerfully positive early mothering. They all had a recollection of really being cared for. Some of these people smoked, some drank, some did both, but few reported having been promiscuous. They almost all seemed to have enjoyed intimacy. They may have been reluctant or embarrassed to speak of sex, but it was easy to see they enjoyed it.

Courtship is a vital part of successful marriage in Western societies. For both men and women it is an assessment of the safety the other person provides. Both sexes require a degree of security in order to relinquish control to the degree that orgasms require. In previous times, times with far lower cancer rates, the romance of courtship was there before the sex. In every "successful" long-term marriage I encountered, romance started in courtship and continued. Occasional flowers, an unsolicited gift, a favorite food prepared, surprises, and parties—all were there for these fortunate people.

Typically the male was more materially giving. I believe this was and is a natural function of convincing a woman that he is "safe," both literally and figuratively, to open up to. When such gestures are looked on as hokum or sexism, part of a loving relationship either never gets started or dies. Giving and accepting are what courtship is about. The opportunity to size up the future partner as a caretaker or potential enemy is what courtship has provided us with throughout the ages.

3

The First Year of Marriage

FOR THE RELATIVELY FEW the honeymoon seems never to end. They remain passionately and almost totally bonded or fused to each other throughout their unusually long lifetimes. For the vast majority, the end of the honeymoon brings the beginning of the marital conflicts that were hidden by the infatuations and passions of courtship. Sometimes it starts almost as the couple passes over the threshold as they recapitulate the aberrations of the mother-baby bonding that both partners experienced at the beginning of life. To understand this we must briefly discuss the earlier stage of development.

The baby is born into a hypersensitive state. Almost all adults appreciate this fact and protect their young from being overstimulated. The protection against outside irritations, for example such things as loud noises, chemicals, or bright sunshine, is consciously attended to by both parents. Intuitively we all know (and people have always known) not to overwhelm a newborn with irritation. But there are irritations from the inside against which defense is not easily accomplished. The baby is growing in almost all its organ systems at a fantastically rapid rate. The only time this rate of growth is again activated in later stage children or adults is during healing (broken bones or wounds) or during *cancerous* cell reproduction.

This growth may be very irritating and, some experts believe, painful. The natural need of the newborn to have hunger removed and the need for elimination certainly seem to be irritants to anyone who has observed newborns. Obviously we cannot protect our babies from such internal irritants as we can from the external (bright lights, chemicals, loud noise). But not so obviously we can reduce their impact by picking up, soothing, rocking, and making reasonable attempts to decrease the internal irritants (like feeding a hungry baby). Everyone has witnessed that almost always the mother is the best one to do this. Baby settles down fastest and most securely with her. The question remains, why? Why is it that babies respond to their mothers so differently than to almost anyone else? The answer is the mother-infant bond. Let me explain.

After mom became pregnant, her body came under the influence of all sorts of biochemical changes. Hormones were produced to help the cell division in mom's body that would permit the developing baby to have a safe implantation in the womb, to allow the structure of pregnancy to form (the thickened uterine wall, the amniotic sac, the cervical plug, placenta, and so forth) and to change the breast tissue to permit milk production. At the same time these hormones did something less scientifically observable but certainly noticed by almost every man and woman who has gone through a pregnancy. The woman's nervous system becomes hypersensitive. Smells and tastes that never bothered her suddenly do. Noise and bright lights may become conspicuously irritating. Mood swings with real joy followed by real downs are not uncommon. Crying at times for no discernible reason is all part of this phenomenon called pregnancy. Certainly contentment and real happiness can be and is frequently part of the same process. The urgently important point is that her nervous system is becoming much like a newborn baby's.

When the baby is born it is a bundle of rawness. The new mother is also still very sensitive and obviously somewhat physically irritated from the birth process. Babies sense feelings much the way dogs or emotionally disturbed adults can frequently sense things. It is an ethereal but observable phenomenon. When mommy's system continues to be like baby's, a fusion or blending together occurs that reduces internal irritation in the baby. It gets shared and diluted with her system.

With Walter and Hannah the internal irritation (carcinogens) of grief were shared, diluted, and dissipated when they lost a son and then a daughter. Walter and Hannah's system blended together. So too does a newborn and his or her mother. The systems in both cases are very similar.

When a problem occurs in bonding, the entropic system, which siphons off biochemical irritation, not only does not work efficiently, it actually backs up. The baby's almost extrasensory awareness of mom's feelings makes it susceptible not only to soothing feelings but also to maternal backups. If the mother is not properly cared for (by her husband and extended family) physically and emotionally, she will rapidly become irritated with any baby. It has been demonstrated time and again that maternal isolation breeds abuse. The baby's cries and discomfort will cause the mother's nervous system to be overloaded if she does not have someone to help siphon off her irritation. After repeated exposure to this now irritated mom, the baby's nervous system gets conditioned to expect irritations. Later in life, anxious people feel actually comforted by the irritating chemicals in a cigarette. Others cannot stop picking scabs or sores. In other words, people become prisoners of the conditioning of added irritation to irritated states. The pattern gets laid down in the earliest stages of life.

Mother represents the world to this very tiny person; the baby's needs and very survival are dependent upon her. Later in life the world will represent mom. Viewing the world as a safe, caring place, or conversely as a frightening, cold place, can easily be seen as directly relating to a mother who was safe and caring or frightening and cold. Phobic reactions, anxiety states, even schizophrenia can be traced back to this earliest learning (see *The Causes and Prevention of Cancer*). Marriage will inevitably evolve into an intense representation of this earliest mother-infant bond.

Going through with a marriage ceremony is really a means of reinstituting a mother-infant and birthing bond for both partners. As previously stated, the vows almost speak of just this type of relationship. The honeymoon can then represent the joy of holding, smelling, touching, tasting, and seeing their newborns for the first time. Or it can represent a postpartem depression. In the mother-baby dyad, if the mother cannot fuse, she will be rejecting the baby to one degree or another. The more depressed she is the more rejecting she will appear to be. Postpartem depression is an indication of an inability to fuse (see *The Causes and Prevention of Cancer*).

After the birth of a marriage, this sudden and usually unexpected inability to fuse is often represented by a horrendous honeymoon experience. The cries of "Why did I marry her?"; "How did I wind up with a jerk like this?" sound remarkably similar to the childhood cries of "Why was I ever born?" They are saying the same thing. How did I wind up with a maternal relationship like this?

(Let me take a moment to address classical psychoanalysis' prejudice against motherhood. If a child or adult develops any emotional problems in response to his or her social environment, the mother is consistently blamed. Her inadequate support systems, husband and extended family, are rarely seen as playing any part. It is true that the first experiences in life will predispose an individual for later physical and emotional symptoms. But where psychoanalysis and psychology in general fail to be honest or at least equitable is in not recognizing the overwhelmingly competent jobs most mothers do. Granted, no one can do a perfect job as a mother. To help women relinquish some of their guilt if their children are not perfect, let's ask some important questions: Have the children done time for being major coke dealers? Have they sustained wounds running guns into Latin America? Have they been married four or five times? On the other hand, do they attend school regularly? Do they relate to friends? Are they successfully employed or married or trying to be? If the answers to the first three questions were "no" and the last three "yes," a woman's mothering abilities should be appreciated. Psychoanalysis emphasizes the problems. It owes an apology to mothers in general for being so unappreciative of the almost impossibly difficult job of mothering.)

Fortunately honeymoons can also be euphoric. The intense romance and hypersexuality may very well be representative of the mother's inability to put her baby down. The baby's need to be held and cuddled also fits into this analogy.

But when this reaction does not get triggered during the honeymoon, the nervous systems of both partners are jarred. If one (or both) partner has a need to push away and be isolated, there will be biochemical consequences. Adrenaline will most likely be elevated as the involuntary nervous system remains poised for flight or fight. The honeymoon may rapidly turn into a pattern of fighting and rejection.

Desperate telephone calls to mother are a sometimes comic but clear indication that infantile feelings are being activated. Mommy should suddenly be able to teach adequate bonding or provide an escape from the closeness that the daughter or son cannot tolerate with the new mother substitute.

Most of the time in this age of liberal sexual attitudes, people do not go through any major sexual shocks on the honeymoon as their parents or grandparents may have in the past. Instead, the specialness of the introduction to permissible sexual intercourse is not there since they probably had intercourse before marriage.

If it also happened with different partners, their feelings cannot help but be less intense. However, if a fusional relationship does appear, the honeymoon may very well still represent the birth of a relationship. Having sex with many different partners does not totally rule out making love for the first time.

This, however, is likely to be the exception to the rule. All too often there is little or no heightening of romantic feelings. There is no birthing of the marriage. There may even be a sense of dullness and depression, a feeling of "what's the big deal, little or nothing is different." These depressive feelings are first learned in infancy and can continue for a lifetime. This type of depression, the depression of pushing away and fearing closeness, of holding things in, or fearing being vulnerable is tragically very common in America. Cancer is also tragically very common in America. Many experts agree that this type of depression correlates to cancer. Every cancer patient I have treated has had this dynamic as part of his or her personality. Thus, honeymoon reactions may warn of the precancerous personality.

Assuming the newlyweds did not live together in a state of quasi-marriage prior to marriage, the sudden increase in the amount of time spent together may be overwhelming. The celebration of the birth of the marriage, and the concurrent licensing of the infantile feelings, come to a partial close when both partners return to their vocations. The time spent together becomes less. Reactions to this may vary from eagerly anticipating the daily reunion to eagerly anticipating getting rid of the new spouse for the time one is at work.

WILL IS THE antithesis of the connotations of his name. Instead of being tall and lanky, he is relatively short with a muscular, stocky physique. At the age of twenty-seven he began working in the aerospace industry as an engineer. He has completed a master's degree. To supplement his income, Will does suburban tree removal jobs. He is married to Alexis, a twenty-four-year-old banking management trainee. She is also the antithesis of what her name connotes. Instead of being snobbish and aloof, Alexis is warm, passionate, and unpretentious. They entered treatment two months after their honeymoon had ended. Alexis initiated the idea because she saw difficulties arising. Will reluctantly went along with the idea because he was tormented by a pressing need to get away from her, to end the marriage and get back to other women.

"She drives me crazy. Every hour on the hour for five months she wants me to tell her I love her. She is all over me. As soon as we get home. I mean I really liked it at first, but she hasn't slowed down at all. She can't get enough of me, and I feel like she is smothering me. No matter how much I tell her I love and care for her this insecure woman demands more. Finally it gets to the point where I am yelling. Can you imagine angrily screaming at someone that you love them? It's bizarre. I end up shouting, 'I love you.' Of course at this point I feel anything but love for her. I feel like grabbing her throat and killing her, that's what I feel.

"If I sit down to watch TV she's all over me. I know most of the guys at work laugh when I complain about this, but they really have no idea what it's like to have a woman who is so clingy and insecure. She must be really insecure to need so much reassurance. I feel drained to the point that I'm beginning to feel that being married to Alexis is like serving a jail sentence. That is, I feel like I won't be able to spend a lifetime married to someone who I just want to get away from as soon as I'm with her. Oh sure, she was like this before we got married, but I figured it would end when we got married. It was reasonable for me to assume that marrying her would end her insecurities, wasn't it? Well, I was dead wrong! She got more and more needy as time went on. I've actually gotten to the point of pushing her away every once in a while. I feel shitty after I act like that, but she gets me to do it.

"From her point of view I'll bet she tells you how cold and disinterested I am. She probably sees me as becoming different after we got married. I guess we both did. I did become less accepting of her after a while. But how much can anyone take?"

Will's mother died when he was less than a year old. His maternal grandmother moved in, and he thinks of her as having been his mother. His father was very inattentive and remarried when Will was six. From that point on it was clear that grandma was no longer welcome, but she was not about to leave her beloved Will. She died of cancer in that home when he was eight. His stepmother quickly evolved into the stereotype: harsh, sadistic, and rejecting. Will has so terrible a history that it amazes me that he functions as well as he does. The mere fact that he lost his mother before the age of seven places him in a high-risk category of developing cancer at some point relatively early in life. Add to this the subsequent loss of his next maternal figure, and we can see why he finds Alexis's need for constant closeness so irritating.

Could he be afraid of losing anyone he really loves? Could he be afraid of being left to stew in his own biochemical juices? Could he have learned to deny his own need for closeness as a way of not again having to face a loss of love? On the surface Will does appear to be a cold, disinterested young husband, but beneath the surface we can see the petrified baby trying desperately to survive. If he does not permit a thorough attachment to Alexis, he cannot be as hurt if she is lost.

But what of Alexis? Is she as clinging and smothering as Will describes? The answer is yes. Alexis was raised by an alcoholic mother, herself a constant infant. No matter how baby Alexis cried, it fell on drunk ears. She has not stopped crying or trying to get what she did not get from a mother who at times slept through her infant's upsets. She married a man whose inability to bond replicates Alexis's mother's inability to bond. We are all prisoners of the familiar. Even when we know what is best for us, we frequently cannot do it! This is due to the overpowering conditioning of the involuntary nervous system in earliest infancy (see *The Causes and Prevention of Cancer*).

If Will does offer some elements of bonding or fusion, Alexis must push the situation until it reproduces the aberrations of bonding from her infancy.

"I don't understand what he wants from me. Does he want me to be a cold bitch who doesn't care? Does he want me to find someone else? I don't know, I just don't know!

"Before we were married Will never complained about my being too affectionate. He never complained when I started cuddling. As soon as we came back from Italy [the honeymoon] he changed. He changed like Dr. Jekyl and Mr. Hyde. If I went near him he was strange—distant, distracted, just plain disinterested. Come to think of it he was weird in Italy too. There we were, on the Amalphi Way, staying in places like Positano. It was so romantic. There was a feeling of the antiquity of these places. Will seemed overwhelmed, but I thought it was due to his feelings for these places and buildings with such a depth of time. Gradually I became aware that he was overwhelmed by me. The more I sensed this the more frightened I became. I mean imagine going on your honeymoon, and gradually it seems your husband doesn't know you exist. I watched him to see if there was a sudden interest in other women. There were very beautiful Italians, Germans, and other Americans, but he wasn't looking at them. He was spacing out on me and the whole world.

"We got back to our routine and started to decorate the apartment. I worked really hard, and he did almost nothing. I painted, and he watched TV. I hung wallpaper, and he ate. He did nothing but complain about being tired. Tired my ass. All he did was sleep, eat, and shit. He was like a baby. That's right, I married a goddamn baby. He moped around a lot and was almost no fun. He was getting depressed. Imagine how that made me feel. I mean I am a newly wedded woman entering into heavenly matrimonial bliss, and my husband is becoming a space cadet. The more I pushed for loving and any contact at all, the further out to Saturn he went. When he passed Jupiter I figured it was time we got help. Don't get me wrong, I know I was clingy. I was getting starved for affection. He said I never left him alone, and he was right. But I feel like he is still slipping away, so what am I supposed to do?"

Alexis was told to back off. It was pointed out that her tactics were making no headway with the problem. In sessions with both of them, they were encouraged to discuss what they wanted from each other. They couldn't. All they could do was complain about what they did not want. The relationship was immersed in negativity—the same type of frustrations and pain they were exposed to at the beginnings of their lives. It took a concerted effort to get them to state things positively. When they finally did, it was clear they both wanted to be loved and accepted. The difficulty remained because Alexis wanted it through constant reassurance and Will through being given his "space."

What appears to be working is treating them as individuals and treating the marriage as a separate "patient." With individual treatment, the infantile reactions stored in their nervous systems are accessible. The analyst is the surrogate mother, and they ascribe the role of inadequately or negligently bonded mother to him. Then he can respond in a corrective way. The "heat" (infantile irritation) is being directed at the therapist instead of each other. At the same time Alexis is doing her best to back off. Will is doing his best to force himself to be more affectionate and aware of his wife. The analyst realizes that these first-aid measures are superficial, but hopes they will change behavior just enough to change some feelings. Waiting for the analytic process to change the feeling could very likely take too long—the marriage could die.

When treatment is not available, a very deliberate do-it-yourselves approach should be attempted. It is very difficult in a situation such as this one, but it is far better than maintaining the infantile patterns.

Unfortunately it is more typical for the individuals to maintain their anger and hurt feelings rather than become determined to make things better. Frequently one partner denies a problem even exists. And people do learn to put up with bad marriages. A somewhat depressed, lonely hopelessness comes to pervade the relationship. When this happens one partner or both are at greater risk of cancer. Month after month, year after year they remain immersed in a sea of internal biochemical carcinogens. It is almost as if they are addicted. When things can change, the opportunities are frequently overlooked or passed up in order to maintain this addiction to internal chemical irritants. In later chapters I will discuss how not to overlook or pass up such moments in marriage. I will also present approaches to change the relationship successfully.

At the time of this writing, Alexis's and Will's marriage is almost a year old. Both partners are still frustrated, but the situation is greatly improved. Will and Alexis have worked out some compromises they both realize are insufficient improvements. But they are both making honest attempts to resolve their differences. They now even joke at times about these very differences. She now refers to him as Calvin—not for Klein but for Coolidge. He tenderly calls her Miss Hollander (the Happy Hooker). There is little doubt that their humor and desire for treatment indicate that they feel their marriage will work. And it will.

PERHAPS THE MORE common and certainly the more difficult newlywed situation to deal with occurs when both partners actively seek distance and neither one objects. The infantile self-containment mechanisms get activated or continue as they have always been. The wedding ceremony does not appear to stimulate residuals from the original mother-baby bonding stage. Instead each partner has already screened the other and found safety in the mutual inability to relate. The newlyweds experience no distress, but both are likely to suffer from chronic feelings of depression. They will not enjoy things as others do. They will be described by neighbors as nice, quiet people. They are plain and simply bland. This chronic depression with a lack of fusion is dangerous. The oomph, the pizazz, the soul, or chutzpah is missing from them as a twosome. They are more like toddlers who are involved in what child psychologists refer to as parallel play.

Before children can adequately interact or share they pursue things in a singular way. They will be peripherally aware of their companions, but the block tower will be built by one child while the other plays with HeMan figures or Cabbage Patch dolls. They may occasionally talk or even watch what the other is doing, but they continue to pursue their own separate ends. If one child does infringe upon another, more often than not he will be greeted with a fit of rage accompanied by striking and/or crying. By the age of three or four, in most cases, children give up this pattern of parallel play. They begin to be partners or opponents in the symbolic representation of life that we commonly call play.

In newlyweds, parallel play can be represented by totally separate interests. Parallel play in adulthood could better be called parallel isolation. A clear example of it is when the couple welcomes separation to give "breathing space." He may paint and wallpaper, and she may be outside gardening or vice versa. Both are more than content with the arrangement. When children come, he may be detached and make no adjustments to his routines, and she may not object in the least. As a matter of fact, this pattern may continue for the duration of their marriage. After all, they are not the least bit aware that there is anything wrong. If one develops a malignancy, the marital relationship is never suspected of contributing in any way. On several occasions I have witnessed cases where both parallel isolates had histories of cancer. It has also been reported to me by colleagues throughout the United States.

Both partners are clearly separate and distinct people. Friends and relatives have a difficult time thinking of them as a couple, as a fusional unit. She plays tennis; he plays golf. She's still into Led Zeppelin, and he thinks nothing can compare to Vivaldi's Four Seasons. When they have sex, they have sex. They do not feel a blending together. Instead they may pursue separate orgasms almost as if they are using the other to masturbate. They roll over and go to sleep with perhaps a mere parting pleasantry.

If they experience an upset, a physical illness or disorder, a setback in their lives, the other will appear to be there for them. But in reality, what the partner offers will be slightly out of sync. They will offer soothing in the face of the irritations of life, but it will be just off target, just not right. The irritated partner would not expect anything else. If the irritated partner received real understanding, he would be genuinely uncomfortable without having the vaguest idea why. The why would be that this fusional experience has probably never been experienced before. The why would be due to a feeling of closeness that represents not just discomfort, but even danger. The why would be because as an infant, closeness to mother meant closeness to a source of real biochemical irritation. The why is because a feeling of blending, of melting into another human being is totally foreign.

DIANE AND ED came back from their honeymoon to set up a home in Suburbia. For almost the entire summer he had Fridays off from his job as a U.P.S. deliveryman. Diane was not sure what she wanted to do as a career, but was considering continuing teaching elementary school for the two years before they would have their first child.

The new house was a modest ranch on a corner plot: lots of grass to cut, to edge, big flower beds to maintain—many chores. Diane is an outdoors person. Ed feels he gets enough exposure to earth, wind, and sun's fire on his job. He handles carpentry, plumbing, painting, and papering. They eat meals together most of the time when they are at home. They discuss what they are each doing. Ed really doesn't care that she wants to plant a European mountain ash or a white birch in the middle of the pachysandra patch at the northern corner of their property. He's not even sure what a European mountain ash looks like. Diane cannot get excited over what stain he is going to use on the shelving he just completed in the den. When Ed speaks of the benefit of spending the money on copper piping versus plastic or aluminum, she does not comprehend or follow what he is saying. She is, however, a very intelligent person.

This is the style, the character of their relationship in general. They are there, and they are not there at the same time. Diane is a racquetball champ. She enters league play and has met several nice friends this way. Ed shoots trap when she plays racquetball. He can usually bust fifty to one hundred straight from the sixteen-yard line. He's good—not great, but really good. He, too, enters league competitions. He joined a gun club after some of the locals saw how good he was. He, too, has made friends through his recreation.

They each introduced the other to their hobbies or sports, but the interest lasted for a couple of months only. While they were both good at the other's primary recreation and encouraged each other, they both decided not to spread themselves too thin. Diane returned to racquetball exclusively, and Ed continued to shatter clay pigeons. With a little help and introspection, they both might have been able to recognize their need to lead separate but parallel lives. They might have been able to see that they share almost nothing that has meaning to them as individuals.

Sex is very much the same—bland. Yes, they have read *The Joy of Sex,* and they have even tried different things. They still change positions, but it follows a regime like a drill team, i.e., him on top, her on top, etc. They have no apparent hang-ups about anything in foreplay. The oomph is just missing. They enjoy it,

70

but it's by the numbers. It is not spontaneous; it does not flow; it lacks humor or adventure.

If Ed reaches over and grabs Diane during a weekend lunch break, they may occasionally wind up having sex. If they do, they wind up in the bedroom—always. They have never made love in any other room. A sense of urgency, of real need, never accompanies their attempts at lovemaking. They have sex. They do not make love. They have only been married eleven months, and many people would see their sexual relationship as dull. Many actually do see that their marital relationship in general is dull. Other couples seem to sense that something is slightly out of sync with them. It makes people uncomfortable although they don't know why. What Diane and Ed both don't know is that without a fusional relationship in life they are at far greater risk of many psychosomatic disorders, including cancer.

REBECCA AND ANGELO are the antithesis of Diane and Ed. They have been married for eight months. It appears that like Hannah and Walter the honeymoon will never stop. Angelo is a surgical resident at a county hospital. Becky is completing her doctorate in clinical psychology. They do not have a lot of time on their hands. The apartment they moved into gets slowly improved upon. It's not a priority. What is a priority is studying together. What is unique is that a clinical psychology student now understands the basics of abdominal surgery and that a surgical resident has learned the fundamentals of learning theory, developmental psychology, and reflective techniques. He can now deal more effectively with his patients' fears and appreciate the importance the mind plays in the areas of endocrinology and neuroimmunology. They are learning from each other because they are interested and appreciate each other.

When Rebecca met Angelo in a medical school library, she was smitten. One look at those dark eyes, his broad shoulders, and

71

lean physique in his hospital greens and she knew. She boldly approached him to ask if he knew where she might find anything on the topic of attitude and healing. He didn't, but he spent over half an hour looking with her. Normally he let nothing but a patient interfere with his study time. This time he let auburn hair, turquoise eyes, and a figure like Raquel Welch distract him. It continued over coffee. Dinner was out because of scheduled surgery, but lunch the next day followed. They did not touch for two weeks. They talked, trying to impress each other, but it was a silly exercise. They both saw this, laughed at it, and then had fun. After a day of horseback riding, they went back to her apartment and they kissed and touched each other. Intercourse was two dates later, again after riding. Angie fell when his horse refused to jump. He was showing off. He let her play doctor by dressing the abrasion on his left thigh. Her hands kept traveling, and that was it.

They thought they had a problem when they recognized that they were definitely going to marry. Angelo is of Italian-Catholic descent, and Becky is of middle European-Jewish descent. They expected problems with their families but received none. Her parents couldn't have been happier: a doctor, a surgeon, and looks like a movie star. His parents saw how gentle and kind she is. One look at her beauty and their son's reaction to her and their objections vanished.

At the time the TV show "Hill Street Blues" was a new sensation. Rebecca's affectionate name for her love thus became "Pizzaman." Angelo called her his bagel, something to do with being Jewish was a lovable orifice. They shared everything from exams to dissertations.

After a tough shift at the hospital she was always there to rub his neck, to offer a warm smile, to just be there when he could not talk. When her tension boiled over from certification exams or research proposals having to be redone and redone, he was equally devoted to soothing and comforting her.

Sex continues to be an adventure. They frequently shower or bathe together. There are two horses who could use Angelo and Becky to explain sex to their colts and fillies. The meadow was just too secluded, too beautiful, and far too tempting. On several occasions after being married, they could not make it out of their car before their passion was satisfied.

When Becky had to take her comprehensive oral exams and defend her dissertation, she was so frightened it scared Angelo. He prepared a candlelight dinner, picked her up, and carried her to bed. In the middle of lovemaking, without her noticing, he put on toy Groucho Marx glasses, nose, and moustache. When she did finally notice she could not stop laughing for ten minutes. What a wonderful tension release humor is. Neither reached orgasm, but neither cared. She breezed through her exams the next day. She could now realize what was really important in her life—him, and them, above all else. Certainly their professions matter to them both, and there are intrinsic stresses. But having a fusional relationship put things into perspective. No matter what seems to happen they can call for mommy and mommy is there. This was true at the beginning of their lives and it is true now.

One important sidelight is that though they are both exceptionally good-looking people, neither one is the least bit jealous or frightened of ever losing the other to another. Their problem, if it is a problem, is in recognizing anyone else exists besides the patients they work with and each other. They make most of their friends feel happy to be with them although some are uncomfortable that their own relationships cannot compare.

LET'S STOP FOR a moment and consider the previous examples. We have marriages like Angelo's and Rebecca's, like Hannah's and Walter's. We have also couples like Will and Alexis, like Paula and Jeff. Does it take five years and five million dollars to do an adequate study to show that the biochemistry of the individuals in the first set of couples will markedly differ from the internal chemical environment of the latter set? Does anyone really doubt that how we interact in our most meaningful relationships will affect our health in general? I think not. People argue and fight in marriages: How they do it as opposed to what they are fighting over is the crucial point. Subsequently we will discuss how to manage such situations. But just consider how many times you have heard people state that their spouses were killing them. Perhaps they were even more specific and declared that he or she "is going to give me cancer." The blame cannot be laid on a marriage for setting up the individual for cancer. To get its start, cancer goes back to the infantile stages. But prevention through marriage *can* help reduce risks by moderating the internal chemical environment in both partners.

Religions have set guidelines for an anti-cancer life-style since their inception. Organized religions of all faiths have recognized the importance of the sanctity of marriage and the integrity of the family as life preserving. They all frown upon divorce and adultery. They emphasize comfort in the biologically determined roles. Religions seem to understand the significance of relating as a means of dissipating irritation. A sense of belonging is their cornerstone.

Several years ago a nine-year-old boy of Arab descent was in a coma suffering from an advanced brain tumor. He lived in California. His last request was granted by an organization whose function is to do just that for dying children. He asked to see his grandmother who at the time was living in Lebanon. She was flown in. Almost immediately as she sat with him, perhaps touched and soothed him, his tumor began to shrink. The newspapers claimed it became of operable size. I hope things worked out well: The newspapers stopped the coverage suddenly. But the tumor did shrink when grandma showed up. When asked why, physicians answered that it was a miracle. A miracle. Their answer was that it was a miracle! Did anyone draw blood from the boy and his grandma to see what was happening endocrino-

74

logically? Did they do white cell counts in both people? The answer is no! We passed up the chance to study this miracle as we have so many others. Perhaps we need a medical specialty of miracology to get "science" to pay attention.

What this example does show is that there are documented cases of cancer being reversed by some significant relationship. All of us know that having a marital relationship like Hannah and Walter or Angelo and Rebecca is life sustaining. Let's stop denying how important it really is.

4

Sex—From an Infantile
Point of View

DISCUSSIONS OF SEXUALITY in books tend to read as if written by a very embarrassed medical school professor or a 42nd Street hooker. Language itself limits the connections made by feelings and sex. We can all at least imagine a sufficiently satisfying sexual experience that "defies description." We have been or can picture lovers so moved that words would somehow break the spell.

In order to discuss sex and love in ways that are meaningful, candor is required. To get to the connections between sexuality and cancer we must be totally honest. The role that sex plays in the development or prevention of cancer is just now beginning to be appreciated by the "scientific" community. I am convinced that adequate marital relationships can help prevent or possibly help in reversing cancers. For this reason sexuality and relating are key points in this book. So, in the immortal words of Joan Rivers, "Can we talk?" If not, skip this chapter. It's not going to pull punches.

The reason that truly satisfying sex defies description is that the feelings experienced bring us back to a developmental time before the use of language or thought. Lovers who can fully enjoy each other will have all their senses stimulated. Touching, seeing, hearing, smelling, and tasting will all be part of any exceptionally satisfying experience. The more advanced senses, hearing and seeing, are usually secondary to the senses of touching, smelling, and tasting.

For some people, inhibition or poor self-image may force the lights out. For others the mystery that touching in the dark provides is even more intense than when light is shed on the subject. Again, constant visual exposure may tend to take the mystery out of lovemaking. For both sexes, studies indicate that a partially clad person is usually more stimulating to view than a totally naked one. But more important than sexual inhibitions or mystery is the role that the "chemical" senses play in sex. They are far more intense for most people.

When we were newborns, these senses of taste and smell, along with touch, were far more hypersensitive than they are in most adults. Lower animals maintain this hypersensitivity to chemicals as a survival mechanism. (They also get cancer more easily.) As the newborn human develops, he or she begins to utilize vision and hearing more and more. As these senses increase in awareness, the chemical ones decrease. This all occurs prior to the human beast being able to think or reason. When it comes to mental activity, all newborns can do is to make certain very simple connections and, most important, feel. These connections are like the act of plugging in the involuntary nervous system. They are very simple but so powerful that they may last a lifetime.

Hunger is *felt* as a building up of tension and perhaps pain, followed by a release provided through feeding. The need to eliminate wastes is certainly *felt* as a buildup of tension and, again, perhaps pain, followed by a release. A pattern of seeking stimulation or tension and having it followed by release is thus established right at the beginning of life. Naturally the mothering figure is responsible for the release of the tensions. Feeding is totally within her control. If a problem exists in elimination, then it is her job to make sure things return to normal by adjusting diet or consulting her pediatrician. If all goes well, what all this amounts to is our learning right from the beginning that we can safely rely upon others to gain satisfaction and pleasure. Similarly, later in life, orgasm provides a pattern of building tension followed by release. Orgasm involves the primitive senses, and it is intensely felt the instant it occurs. People do not have to think about it at all. It is mindless in the sense of requiring no reasoning, no abstraction, no nothing but feelings and sensation. It brings us back to the beginnings of our lives.

There are other indications that sexuality is connected to the beginning of life. We would want our lovers to be the kind of mother who could know our needs without our asking (prelanguage). We would all want a lover who could manipulate our bodies to reduce the excitement level of preorgasm tensions with a "mind shattering" (prethought) orgasm. Ideally lovers should be able to accomplish this without having to be instructed. After all, babies cannot tell their mothers what would feel good. Fortunately, as adults we can communicate our needs to our lovers. But a really sensitive partner who can respond to a lover's reactions and needs without having to be told is a powerful replication of the earliest maternal relationship. This quality of lovemaking would make almost anyone consider such a relationship as very special.

More typical is the relationship that requires verbal sexual communication for both partners to be satisfied. It may or may not actually detract from the loving. If occasional instruction is needed, no harm is done. If there is a need to keep repeating any teaching then one, or maybe both, partner may be perceived as a negligent mother. If the first (infantile) relationship for either or both partners was not fusional, the marital relationship may not fuse, and the partners will not be in touch. Later in this chapter we will discuss getting in touch, perhaps for the first time.

Another important connection of adult sexuality with infancy is that no one offering soothing and comforting to a newborn does it without rocking and swaying. The tie in to the rocking and swaying of people making love or just embracing is clear. Almost anytime people are entranced, in lovemaking or with a musical or religious experience, movement is an important part. Gospel singers are rarely devoid of swaying motions; Jews rock back and forth in the synagogue; and entire mobs of music fans will sway in unison from side to side at a concert. In all of these examples, rocking and swaying provide a bodily sensation that promotes fusional feelings. In the case of religious experience, the fusion is with God; in the case of the musical experience, the fusion is with the performer. God and these highly worshiped stars are always viewed as connected, caring, and concerned. They are perceived as capable and highly competent to meet needs. A bonding is always powerfully desired. Belonging to someone or something is a frequent theme of popular music and, as previously stated, all religions. Movements that replicate the movements of mother-infant bonding are close to universal for anyone experiencing any real feelings of fusion. From the tribes of Africa and America to the temples of Asia to the churches and synagogues of Europe and the United States, people rock and sway to music and religious celebrations. And among these different people, rocking and swaying is an important part of child rearing and lovemaking. This is part of the human experience.

A more powerful connection between sex and infancy brings us to the topic of oral sex. Oral sex is commonly practiced throughout the world as part of normal foreplay and as a means to orgasm. Higher-level mammals will frequently engage in it to aid in lubrication and to make females more receptive for intercourse. It is thus difficult to see it as an act against God's will. In reality, oral sex is reported by many people surveyed as being even more intimate than intercourse. It can bring us back to the intensity of taste and smell as infantile fusion is reawakened.

People passionately lost in the act of oral sex are provided with the opportunity to regress to levels where stimulation of the mouth was the primary form of pleasure and gratification. This level was the first stage of life. Oral sex can provide access to a very good symbolic maternal breast. Well before Sigmund Freud, Charles Darwin wrote, "In our maturer years when an object of vision is presented to us which bears any similitude to the form of the female bosom we feel a general glow of delight which seems to influence all our senses, and if the object be not too large we experience an attraction to embrace it with our lips as we did in early infancy the bosom of our mothers."

For males, sucking on female breasts is an obvious connection to infancy. America's obsession with the female breast indicates an almost national interest in continuing what was good or looking for what was perhaps not there. When the male performs oral sex on his partner's genitals, sucking and licking are his obvious means of pleasing her. The natural scent of the female's genitals is highly stimulating for almost all men who enjoy such close contact.

There are, however, people who have great difficulty appreciating the female genitals. If a woman feels that her internal system is somehow "dirty" she will be uncomfortable with oral sex, and her partner may feel rejected in response to her feelings. If, however, *he* feels her vaginal area is dirty or is repulsed by it, for whatever reason, she will feel rejected. Such rejections are tremendously destructive to the total acceptance a fusional marriage requires.

The female partner's oral performance is a bit more confusing in terms of relating it to infancy. The penis is worshiped in many societies. Much art is devoted to it throughout the world. Many women such as Paula candidly admit a loving fascination with the male organ. Melanie Klein, a famous psychoanalyst, postulates the idea that the penis can be viewed as a substitute maternal breast. Again, remember that everyone, male and female, marries his or her earliest mother figure, and the breast was most important to the newborn boy or girl.

The adult male breast is rarely considered a highly erotic site of sexual pleasure for either partner. An attractive male chest is usually thought of as being hard and muscular, not exactly maternal-like. The penis, while certainly hard and firm, still has the soft and smooth head. However, if a woman associates the phallus with elimination, or if that first breast was symbolically toxic, then the penis will be given a negative association. She may balk at the act of oral sex. This will then lead to feelings of rejection. I have treated men who were involved in adulterous relationships with prostitutes, co-workers, or whomever, for the sole purpose of receiving oral gratification.

Jerry is one of them.

"I love my wife, but sex with us is the pits. She always was shy and embarrassed, and I should have known. After our fourth date when we went back to my apartment, things got going and we finally wound up naked on my couch. I kissed her breasts, licked her neck and ears, I even kissed and licked the bend in her arms and behind her knees. I wanted her crazy for me before I went down on her. But I could tell she was tense. I slowed down and became very gentle. I was barely licking her when she came. Then I guess she felt obligated to suck me.

"I could tell instantly that this was not her forte. After she gagged a lot, she looked up and said, please don't come in my mouth! That's okay with me, but she just kept on gagging. She was obviously repulsed. I should have known then. Blow jobs are very important to me. Sex without them is like golfing with only a putter. After we were married I figured I could patiently teach her. She's got a problem. Let me tell you, she does. If any of my semen gets on her hand she reacts like it was poison or acid or something. She washes right after sex, no cuddling, just washing. Oh, it's not that she doesn't try. She does, but she can't get past it. I feel sorry for her. But I am not about to go through the rest of my life without oral sex.

"As soon as Chris started as the receptionist at work I knew she'd be terrific. She's twelve years younger than me and is gorgeous. She dresses properly at work, but this girl is a walking erector set. We went out to lunch with some others, and I could tell she was eyeballing me. I knew, somehow I knew this girl loved oral sex. I just knew, don't ask me how.

"We met for dinner a week later and wound up at her apartment. We started dancing and of course we had sex. She was naked to the waist and pulled my penis out of my pants. Then she went down on me and I mean I thought I died and went to heaven. When I came she not only didn't flinch, she acted like it was ambrosia. But when I tried to please her, she couldn't reach an orgasm. After several dates I became aware that she orgasmed when she blew me. But that was the only way she could.

"So here I am married to a woman who can enjoy sex if I handle her like Dresden china and having an affair with a woman who cannot allow me any active way of pleasing her. There is no feeling of exchange with either one. My wife acts as if my penis was disgusting, and my girlfriend acts as if it were the reason for her existence. I'm not about to give up either one, but I wish they could be combined into one. Then that female would be perfect. I guess I could go through my life being frustrated, but I don't see where I have a choice. Maybe I should keep looking for someone who can do me right. Anyway how did I wind up in such a crazy set of circumstances?"

This crazy set of circumstances—looking for women who could satisfy and somehow winding up frustrated regardless—certainly is not unique. Over and over again mental health professionals observe this pattern. A divorce occurs, and both partners marry the clone of the person just divorced. The behavior of the clone may differ, but the feelings in the new relationship remain the same. The need to repeat what is familiar is a powerful compulsion in all of us.

The answer to Jerry's question can be found by tracing back to a mothering experience where the roles were reversed. Right from the beginning of life Jerry got the message that he was treading on thin ice, dealing with Dresden china. His mother was extremely inconsistent. He never got what he expected but quickly learned that he got only what she was willing to give. Another out-of-touch mother-infant bond. By the time he was school age, his mother had become relatively unimportant in his life. He continued to expect to be frustrated, but he kept hoping that he would get what he always should have gotten. He did well in school and was surprised that his mother never seemed pleased by this. He moved up in business to become a partner in a construction firm. Still no appreciation. He wound up marrying a woman who, like his mother, made him feel unaccepted and unappreciated. In his affair, Chris made him feel the same way in spite of her enjoyment in performing oral sex. She could not accept orgasms unless she was in total control of the situation. While it might appear that Chris was only out to please him, in reality, she was just as depriving as his wife.

Jerry has few or no sexual inhibitions. But he does have a need to achieve and be appreciated. Assuming that he really enjoys pleasing a woman, Chris's inability to be so pleased would have to be seen as rejecting.

Jerry's wife, by the way, does have a name. It is interesting how rarely he refers to her as "Pam." Perhaps this indicates that on some level he wants nothing, not even a name, to interfere with his view of her as a repetition of his mother. He never described her physical appearance during the course of his treatment. When he speaks of her it is as if she is a nonentity.

After almost a year of analysis, Jerry was able to get Pam to enter treatment. She is a pleasant-looking woman with a pleasingly full figure. Any extra pounds have gone to all the right places. My first impression was that she was like a frightened, sad puppy. I knew I would have to be very careful with her. That left us with almost nothing to say. Her major topic was her desire not to be speaking to me.

Then it finally happened—on "Dallas," J.R. got shot. It was like a champagne cork had popped. The communication flowed and flowed, to the point that she seemed intoxicated by the whole "Dallas" show. Shy, demure Pam told me J.R. was a "son of a bitch." She screamed when she described what a cruel woman-hater this antihero was. Then she would talk about how she would have no problems with a rotten guy like him, that she would delight in taming him. If asked how she would tame him, she returned to being shy, demure Pam.

"Maybe Jerry is just too nice to me. When we got married he was making peanuts, but now he's worth a fortune. He sold his business after several years and started another one. He sold that one two years ago and sort of consults for them or something now. For a guy who never went to college he has done all right. But I certainly was with him before anything like that happened. Without money he was a really nice, gentle man. His gentleness made me feel he was strong. And his strength made me feel safe. Except for, except for in our lovemaking. He was so powerful in all ways, physically, emotionally, intellectually, that I guess I was overwhelmed by him without even knowing it.

"Once when he got angry at me he picked up our German shepherd and threw him across the den. Thank God the dog was all right, but I was even more scared of him after that. He never hit me or anyone else I know of besides Hans, that was the dog. Hans weighed a hundred and thirty pounds. [This is a gentle guy? We can suspect Pam is fraught with contradictions.]

"We're just really different when it comes to sex. I mean I could be happy having it once a week or to be honest even less. I'm not sure I'm interested in it at all. I was brought up that nice girls don't go crazy with sex. I enjoy it when it happens. I just don't do much to make it happen. I enjoy almost everything we do, but it has to be really slow and easy for me."

"He probably told you that I don't like to use my mouth on him. This is very perplexing. I did do that with two other men in my life, before Jerry, of course. With one guy, who my parents really hated, he taught me. And I could do it the way Jerry wants, you know, all the way. Come to think of it, I liked to do that with George, too. But something is wrong when I try to do it with Jerry. I start to feel sick. I can get him aroused that way, but then he has to finish the usual way. I can't figure this out. Jerry would die if he ever knew I did that with other boys before him. I feel guilty about it. He is good to me in so many ways. I mean I try, I really try because I know it is important to him. But I just can't."

"What I can't understand is why it didn't bother me with the other two men I had sex with. There can't be that much difference between different men. So why can't I do it with Jerry.

"Sometimes I do have ridiculous fears that he would look for that elsewhere, you know, another woman. But then I can reassure myself that he is the most ethical man I have ever known. I know my Jerry and I'm pretty sure he wouldn't do that."

Pam unconsciously already knows. She is a woman dedicated to contradictions and denial. She cannot accept the man she sees as ethical and caring. The two other men were relatively brief youthful relationships. They did not trigger the powerful reawakening of feelings that Jerry does.

Pam was born two and a half years after her brother. Her mother was described as being rather frenetic and flighty. The stories of childhood always centered upon what a good, quiet baby she was. And it was clear that her brother was more than her mother could handle. Mom was a woman who never stopped. She was on her feet from sunup to sundown. It is safe to assume that Mom was hyperirritated herself when she finally got to offer soothing and comfort to baby Pam. Thus Pam's nervous system was being set up. The person to connect to would have to duplicate these early patterns. He would have to be overwhelming and somewhat frightening.

Pam unconsciously sees Jerry as fitting the mold. He frightens her even though she has never been directly abused. When he gives in ways that are nonimpinging, she not only accepts but is genuinely appreciative. But an erect penis is meant to intrude, to impinge. It is acceptable from Jerry if it is not impinging in a way that cannot be denied. Intercourse permits Pam to regulate how aroused she wishes to be. She can really let go or totally hold back, deny. Oral sex brings her more clearly back to early infancy, at least with Jerry. His semen, his milk is poison. The other males' semen was just semen. It was not connected to feelings of irritation and fear stored in her nervous system from infancy. Repulsion or disgust are feelings that usually cover intense fear.

This marriage superficially would be seen by most people as quite adequate. Jerry and Pam are polite and kind to each other. They never seem to fight. They enjoy the success they have attained. They even spend a great deal of time together, sharing a love for their forty-two foot boat and the sea. In reality, however, both—Pam perhaps far more so—risk developing cancer.

Pam cannot totally fuse and lose herself to the passions of sexuality. There is no total acceptance of Jerry. She is afraid. She sees him as another J.R., an emotionally negligent, depriving man who can easily attract women who need to repeat a negative early experience. Too late they would find that they were again involved with poison. The excitement would rapidly fade and the poison would be left.

Pam is at greater risk of cancer because Jerry is involved with another woman, and she knows that on some level. Doctors and mental health professionals have written to me to find out if I too have encountered a relationship between husbands committing adultery and wives developing breast cancer. The answer is that I have.

Pam already senses that something is terribly wrong. The more insecure she feels the more elevated her adrenaline and corticosteroids. The more of these chronic internal carcinogens, the greater the risk. So any marriage with adultery will increase cancer risks. Why it is usually breast cancer requires further study. The older schools of psychology suggest that we can all be taught, or forced, to chronically irritate specific organ systems in our bodies. Breasts that are being sexually ignored are one such organ system. Nuns have a significantly high rate of breast cancer. Divorced and widowed women also do. Women who cannot bond or fuse are more vulnerable.

Recent surveys show that almost one out of three men and one out of four women are involved in extramarital sex. Is it a coincidence that the adultery rates and cancer rates in America are almost identical?

Intercourse and oral sex are an important bonding for the majority of Americans. Any aberrations of sexual functioning that leaves one or both marital partners chronically frustrated is carcinogenic. The emptiness, depression, and loneliness that can follow inadequate sexual relations can probably only be rivaled by the loss of a loved one. It is true despair. There is nothing more life sustaining than good, fusional, loving sex.

WHAT IS HAPPENING when a man and woman are in the midst of intercourse? Obviously their genitals are in the most intense contact. But perhaps even more important their entire bodies are embracing. Large portions of skin are being stimulated. A tender or passionate kiss may be part of the act. A rhythmic motion is present. As intense pleasure is building up in the sexual organs, the entire bodies are embracing, swaying, trying to fuse together. The more passionate the experience the more primitive the feelings, the more intense the bonding.

The not very deep or dark secret of really loving and enjoyable sexual intercourse is balance. This balance requires an equality in give and take. When lovers are as equally devoted to pleasing each other as being pleased, the balance is operating. When a mother successfully soothes and comforts her baby, it is hard to tell who is receiving more pleasure. When there is no way to determine who is being more pleased in sexual intercourse, a truly fusional experience is happening. Intercourse provides the opportunity to be mothering and babied almost simultaneously. It is the ultimate taking care of each other.

EVELYN AND JOHN are average people. They are average looking. They were average students. The census bureau and I.R.S. would say they have an average-size family with an average income. On Sundays they and their children attend a Methodist church. On Saturdays they bowl together in a league. Their car is a 1978 slightly rusted green Malibu station wagon. There is a chip in the windshield midway between the driver's and passenger's side. They have an eleven-year-old beagle. Tonto's tail is a nonstop meter of household happiness. Evelyn and John are average people when it comes to everything but love and sex. After nineteen years of marriage, they are even more in love than when they first married.

Their first year was not terrific. They both went through major adjustments. John was somewhat shy and inhibited. He wanted the lights out when making love, not for mystery, but because of his inhibitions. Evelyn had never had another man in her life and most certainly never will. But when she finally made love to John, a switch got turned on that even nineteen years of strict "Christian" upbringing could not keep frozen. John was overwhelmed and afraid of not being sexually adequate. The National Football League might not have been adequate, for Evelyn loved to make love. Every morning, every evening she wanted him. John thought she stopped to eat only in order to keep her strength up. According to his best recollection they once made love eleven times in less than sixteen hours.

"Within six months of marriage, I felt like I needed transfusions. The thought occurred to me that maybe I married a nymphomaniac. Then she seemed to finally notice that I was rapidly dying.

"Any uptightness in me had no chance of surviving. Within the first couple of weeks I got used to the lights being on. I also got used to Evie being on. At first all I felt was the pressure.

"Within a couple of months she was pregnant. We were happy. God, I was happy that she was too pooped to pop. The pregnancy of our first was the best time of my young married life. I got to sleep. After Francis was born things became normal. Actually I was worried that she was no longer interested. Well you have to realize that I knew nothing about what was average sexually. I figured everyone got it on four or five times a day. Now I realize we were newlywed bunnies. The pressure, the urgency behind sex suddenly subsided. After the baby we slowed down to twice or maybe three times a day, most of the time twice. But it was better. It was slower, calmer, more gentle. I fell in love with her all over again. She is like a work of art, really she's beautiful. She still is. I love her legs and ass. She still is lean and firm feeling.

"I love her even more now. That's because I don't feel pressured. Neither one of us are movie star types, but we both enjoy each other. Not just in bed, but also in the alley. We bowl together. She's good at both, but to tell you the truth, I don't really know if she's any good at all. You see, I've never had real sex with anyone else. Evelyn is the only woman I ever did it all the way with. Maybe there are others who would be even better. And maybe there are things we don't know anything about. But we don't care. We are in love, always have been, and always will be. I like certain things better than others, but that's private stuff, you understand. I just love when she rubs my neck and back after a tough day. The kids tease us that we aren't like the other parents. We always touch. Her smile can make the worst in my life far more bearable. I love her sense of humor and her desire to please me. When I turned forty she threw me a surprise birthday party. There must have been a hundred people there. Everyone brought a gift and food. The guys from work and lots of people from the bowling league showed up. They're good people. She makes me feel special all the time though. I hope I do the same for her. Oh, I know I do."

Evelyn reported the same beginnings to the marriage. She was perplexed by her own early reactions.

"I didn't understand what I was feeling when we first got married. I could not stand to be away from him. When we made love it was never enough. A few times I met him at the door naked, and I thought he'd die. His face got all red. I mean I wasn't where anyone could see us, that wasn't it. He was just embarrassed. Sometimes I stripped him before he got to the bedroom. Sometimes we didn't get to the bedroom until after the first or second time. He was so strong that even afterward he did not have to wait. We just kept doing it and doing it. He was nonstop for hours. It was glorious. But what was really glorious was that here I was, a very proper young lady who knew next to nothing. All I wanted to do was make love with him. I really was out of control. The poor boy was so tired that sometimes I didn't have the heart to wake him for more. I just lay awake watching him sleep. He was darling with his messed-up hair. It took real control not to start playing with it. But I knew, at least at times I knew, he wouldn't survive if we kept it up [laughter].

"I don't know what it was, the feeling was to push his whole body into me. Our blood mixed when we made love. I was addicted. When he was at work I thought of him. When we were bowling I thought of making love with him. When we were with friends I wanted them to leave. I thought I had become a sex maniac. But I figured that you couldn't be a sex maniac with your own husband. I figured whatever we wanted and did was okay. We had a real nice church wedding. We got the stamp of approval, and we were taking that approval to the limits.

"We slowed down after the first year, what with being pregnant and then the baby. He was so good with the babies. I fell more in love with him for being such a good man. We still make love almost every day, sometimes more than that. He likes it as much as I do. I can't really describe what happens, but I know it's the reason I'm alive. I still feel like melting when he touches me. I still get excited when he walks into a room. We care for each

91

other. We love our children, friends, and family, but we both know that we'd never make love to any other person as long as we live. We've seen other couples break up, families fall apart, and we're so grateful to God to have each other. There is a feeling when he is with me, well just that I'm safe. For that time nothing else amounts to anything. We blend together, we melt into each other. Anyone who thinks this could happen more than once in their lifetime probably has never had it even once. I know this sounds ridiculous, but I could not live without having John inside me, hugging me, loving me. I know I'd die if anything ever happened to him. I guess I should be scared of being so dependent, but I'm not.

"Every night of our married lives we've had this wonderful feeling of nothing else mattering. As soon as he is in me my mind switches off. I don't care, I can't care about anything else. My entire body tingles. My skin all over is turned on. He once went on a trip with the guys, and I didn't really sleep for four nights. It felt so strange to be in bed without making love to John. Something inside me told me this was not just unpleasant, it was downright dangerous. I'm not kidding. I felt like I was in danger."

Evelyn may be 100 percent correct. How many times have we all heard of situations where one member of a happy marriage dies and the other develops cancer in very short order. We have statistical studies that prove this point. The loss of a love like this must have profound effects on our internal biochemical environment. In such grief reactions the immune system stops working efficiently. We have studies to demonstrate this. But everyone already knows the importance of love and the tragedy of the loss of it. We can now connect it to the onset of cancer.

Perhaps John and Evelyn's hypersexuality at the very beginning of their marriage could have led to difficulties. John was genuinely frightened by it. But he also knew she loved him. This love permitted her to sense his fears and at least partially back off.

Humor and joking were part of their relationship. This is true of the other positive relationships I have cited. Apparently it is another vital component to adequate sexual and loving adjustments. For people like Evelyn and John, Walter and Hannah, Rebecca and Angelo, humor is what made them fun to be with. It added to their charm as couples, but it also allowed for a discharge of internal irritations as they arose. Humor permitted a leveling, a balancing in their interactions. It made them delightful and kept them youthful.

THE EXPERTS TELL us it's all right to say no, but if sex is refused too often, if it occurs too infrequently, we may be dealing with either or both partner's depression. If chronic headache or fatigue is the usual excuse for avoiding sex, then someone is depressed and depressed in a way that correlates to cancers. The constant rejection of sex is rejection at a very basic level.

Solitary masturbation is another way of saying no. Masturbation alone is really very alone. It tends to emphasize the lack of an adequate relationship. It speaks of the baby left literally and figuratively to his own devices, the neglected infant. The discharge of internal biochemical irritations was left up to the infant to manage. The baby inside the adult continues to take care of himself when chronic masturbation is the outlet. Almost everyone masturbates once in a while, but it is no substitute for relating. When solitary masturbation happens more often than sexual relations, it is a symptom of depression.

The apparent opposite of solitary, asexual masturbation is the practice of serial marriage and/or swapping and swinging. The need for multiple partners may also indicate a clear repetition of an inability to bond or fuse. Divorce after divorce is usually referred to as serial marriage. As each relationship reaches the level of intensity of the original mother-infant bond, the infantile depression gets activated to ward off the substitute mother's assumed irritations.

Divorce correlates to cancer. Study after study indicates this fact. Hannah and Walter might have a bone to pick with anyone advocating that changing partners is better than an adjustment to each other over the years. But giving up without doing everything possible seems to be more and more the style of ending marriages. It is dangerous, and in many cases the next marriage is equally bad. The clone gets found, and the feelings are the same.

The Joy of Sex by Alex Comfort advocates that good friends can share each other in multiple sexual experiences. I don't think I have to really explain how antifusional sharing one's spouse can be. It is practiced by people who are so depressed that they need all this stimulation to create a cover of false euphoria. A therapist gets to pick up the pieces when the euphoria ends and the frenetic pace cannot be maintained. The misery here is so overwhelming that depression is an understated description of it. Simply enough, swapping, swinging, and orgies are antifusional.

I know this all sounds reactionary; staying married, limited masturbation, no adultery, no orgies. I'm only advocating sexual and marital practices to promote feeling of the original bonding. I'm convinced those feelings are life preserving. Anything that interferes is carcinogenic.

It is true that some marriages are more likely to cause cancer than divorce. These carcinogenic marriages will be discussed more fully in subsequent chapters.

5

The Care and Feeding
of the Pregnant Human

WHEN IN THE COURSE OF human events a wife convinces a husband (usually) that it is time for a baby, an enormously complex chain of events begins. Every one of these events has the potential of being truly wonderful or miserably horrendous. They begin with the motivation behind the wish to reproduce.

After a relatively brief number of years many married women experience an intense desire for a baby. If the marriage is progressing in ways that increase love, permit a mutual sexual adjustment, and allow for an exchange of caring and soothing, then pregnancy most likely will be experienced as a joyous, loving time. If the converse is true, the foundations for greater problems for the couple and the future child are being laid. Ideally, a woman desires to be pregnant as a clear need to express her biological fulfillment through the ultimate loving bond she can share with her husband.

It is a woman's right to bear children if she is capable and so desires. It is the most creative act any human being can accomplish. At the same time, it merely requires that the plumbing works and a spermatozoa is available. To have a wonderful feeling of being creative usually means the existence of a happy marital relationship.

Frequently psychoanalysts encounter situations where a terrible marriage existed and the pregnancy and birth were naively viewed as a way "to save the marriage." The human mind's ability to deny blatant reality never fails to amaze me. It's not surprising then to encounter young women who, faced with situation after situation in a negative marriage confirming that their husbands are incapable of loving or caring sufficiently to make a marriage work, much less to be a vaguely adequate father, still assume that such a husband will share her desire for a child. She is projecting her own wishes onto him, but, more important, she is already establishing a role reversal with her baby. Instead of the child being born into a world where his or her needs are unconditionally accepted, this child will be born to meet mother's needs. Whenever a baby is born to be used by the mother for some ulterior motive, the foundation of anxiety, chronic worry, and an inability to allow real closeness are being laid down in this infant.

When a woman chooses to conceive in order to prove that she is a woman, we again have the baby being set up. In this day and age, the idea of what constitutes a "real woman" is no longer very clear. Women are in all sorts of previously exclusively male roles. Professionally and in business, women have demonstrated not only their equality but in many specific areas their superiority. Insecure males are easily threatened by females infringing on their protected domains. If the female turns out to be equal or superior, her feminity will be the first thing they will attack.

So we can see how, in our present sex-role turmoil, many women subjected to insecure men begin to believe the accusations and question their own feminity. It is not always a conscious questioning. When it reaches its extreme, a baby is the ultimate proof of feminity. Another pawn enters the world. Another child is reversing roles in life with mother. And another woman finds out that having the right equipment and available sperm does not really prove too much.

Less frequently, women will seek pregnancy after they have accepted not being loved in their marriages. The thought here is that a baby will make it all somewhat tolerable. The baby will meet the emotional needs that the husband is unwilling or incapable of meeting. It is someone to love. Right—reversal again.

The army used to describe eighteen-year-old male babies as suffering from Momism. The bond appeared too tight, but the problem was really one of the son fearing separation from Mom. Leaving her made her somehow vulnerable. School phobics frequently do not fear school. They fear leaving Mom to her own means of protection. They sit in school petrified not about what is happening to them, but rather what is happening in a home where an unhappy marriage exists and they, the buffer, are removed.

I realize this is a loaded topic, but one of the most frightening problems of our nonfusional times is artificial insemination, because so little is known of the psychological and thus long-term biological ramifications. In the procedure where a husband's sperm can be used to fertilize his wife's ova, even if the fertilization is outside of the womb followed by an implantation, there is nothing to which my theory of fusing would object. But when another man's sperm must be used, what effect does this have on the fusional aspects of the marriage? What effect does this have on the husband's self-concept? What effect does it have on his ability to relate to the child? We don't really know.

Would it be easier for most married men to adopt a baby rather than have a strange man's sperm enter their wives' reproductive system? Is the woman who can conceive and is desirous of experiencing a pregnancy, even if her husband is sterile, selfishly putting her needs first? Can one get an honest answer to these questions from any man who has been tested and shown to be sterile? Would guilt and despair cloud his judgment of knowing what his feeling would be after the baby is born? Can artificial insemination with any sperm other than the husband's be anything but antifusional? We don't know.

97

There has been a far more frightening development in recent years. Women who are intentionally or involuntarily lacking a man in their lives are using artificial insemination to become pregnant. Lesbians and women reaching the time limit on their biological clocks are conceiving in this manner. A technical advance emerges, and the idea that a marital dyad is the basis for a family falls by the wayside.

Our technological society is reaching the limits of egocentric absurdity. What if women need men and men need women in order to raise babies correctly? What does it say to a child to be sired by a sperm bank? Yes, some children are born into families with so much conflict that they might very well be better off with just one parent. It is, however, questionable that techniques are being practiced that distort and circumvent what we have always considered to be the family.

CARLA IS THIRTY-SEVEN and recently had a baby. After four years of marriage her husband, Sean, had convinced her that having a baby would be more rewarding than devoting all her time to the business she had opened with her childhood buddy, Edwina. The boutique had grown rapidly, and within five years they each were running a shop at a separate location. Carla is gifted at picking styles from Italy. Her competition cannot compete with her taste. She was even approached by some store owners in Utah and Arizona to do the buying for their shops.

Sean is an architect who has won numerous awards for magnificent designs throughout the Northeast. After they had unsuccessfully tried to conceive for some time, he became clinically depressed when he learned that their inability to conceive was due to his sperm count being very low; the few sperm present were immobile. He was resistant to consolation, but it did not really matter—Carla was too angry and disappointed to offer any.

A year went by, and the marriage almost ended. Sex stopped: At times he couldn't, and at other times she wouldn't. Then

98

Edwina came to the rescue. She had just spoken to a customer who was single and pushing forty. The woman, who had come into the boutique after an absence of almost a year, brought her baby daughter with her. Edwina was a bit taken back, but the customer volunteered the information that she had been artificially inseminated at a California sperm bank supplied with sperm from Nobel prize laureates. She had flown out there to receive this genetic prize. Her mother saw a future Barbara McClintock or Madam Curie in the child. Edwina looked at the two-month-old girl and saw a two-month-old girl and a solution for her dear friend's problem. As soon as the woman left, Edwina called Carla. She was so excited that she got both of them shaking in just moments.

It all sounded great to her, but what of Sean's reaction? Carla prepared a candlelight dinner. Champagne was part of it, and his favorite meal, trout almondine, was served in a style to rival the Four Seasons. Then she told him of Edwina's suggestion. He stormed out of the house. When he had suggested adoption, she had pooh-poohed the idea. Now she wanted to have a baby that would be hers biologically and his adoptively.

In the next few days she explained her pressing need to experience a pregnancy. He at first argued it was one step short of going out and having sex with a (granted very bright) stranger. After several weeks he was sufficiently depressed and spaced out to say yes. He candidly admitted that he felt dead emotionally and that he was not sure how he would relate to "this guy's kid."

She did it. Sean did not make the trip; Edwina went with her. The technique worked, and ten days later she tested positive. During those ten days Sean was a nonstop sex machine. Later he admitted that this way he was able to tell himself, "Just maybe this baby is mine."

The ultimate irony then began to unfold. As the pregnancy progressed Sean began to fall in love with the baby. Carla remained at work and paid almost no attention to her physical condition. She was just slightly more irritable than usual. On the way to the hospital she calmed *him* down. The delivery wound up as a cesarean section, and Carla felt deprived because the pregnancy did not end "normally." She didn't consider the fact that it hadn't started normally either. At this point it did not seem to matter to her. Sean was there for both of them.

After the fifth week Carla returned to work, with a housekeeper and Sean sharing the burden and joy of raising a newborn. At eight months of age little James (named after a respected Nobel laureate in genetics) obviously loved Nanny and Daddy a great deal. He bonded to whoever was available to bond to. Whenever Carla approached he got fussy and irritated. It was an obvious reaction that anyone could observe. Carla grew more and more rejected and rejecting. Finally one evening it slipped out. "I don't understand it. You'd think the blood ties would be stronger. I can't figure out why he can't sense the blood difference with you and me."

Her initial selfishness was now followed by this horrendous attack. She experienced no fusion or bonding with her baby, and she resented Sean's ability to do so. Up to this point even her choice of name had not interfered with his reaction to his adopted son. But this was too much. He left.

Carla's need to destroy the bond was satisfied. The baby had failed to meet her need to prove her femininity. The cesarean section had deprived her of her ultimate test—a vaginal delivery. Her husband had not met her needs, and her son had started off life disappointing her.

This marriage was not good to begin with, but the lack of fusion accompanying the pregnancy has in all probability destroyed it. Loving a baby is wanting a baby, not needing one.

ALONG WITH THE advent of sperm banks and artificial insemination the news media introduced us to the converse: surrogate mothers. For fees, ranging from $10,000 and up, women have accepted through artificial insemination the sperm of men who are married to infertile women. They conceive and carry to full term the husband's offspring. In this case the wife is the one forced to deal with not only her infertility, but the adoptive rearing of her husband's biological infant.

All of the problems of artificial insemination are present now for the opposite partner. Will she be able to fuse and bond adequately? Would it be easier for both of them if the child was adopted? Is there a feeling of imbalance in the relationship due to a blood relationship versus an adoptive one? Again, medical science moves ahead with little or no knowledge of any long-term consequences.

Carla and Sean's experience demonstrates how aberrations of fusion in modern marriage preclude the possibility of fusion in pregnancy or early child rearing. Granted this is an extreme case but it is a real one. It happened. More typically, the antifusional negativity is more subtle. A husband may tell his pregnant wife that she is acting like a baby, or he may feel that she is silly if normal feelings of pregnancy evolve. He may also resent her importance in the process. The most common error in both spouses is an unawareness of or lack of appreciation for the regression that pregnancy stimulates in both of them.

When a woman becomes pregnant the implantation of the fertilized egg triggers a wonderfully complex and intricate chain of biochemical, physiological, and emotional reactions. On a psychological level, they all add up to an increased level of hypersensitivity. As previously mentioned, the enormous influx of hormones helps regulate the formation of necessary pregnancy structures: The uterus enlarges and thickens; the placenta and amniotic sac form; the protective cervical plug forms; and breast tissue begins to change to facilitate milk production. All of these changes are brought about by the irritating effects of hormones that trigger the cells to behave in the necessary ways. At other, nonpregnant times, things like ulcers or fractured bones are

101

irritated into healing by the influence of hormones. Growth in pregnancy for women and babies is based upon this biochemical irritation.

Having all of these hormones flowing through one's body has the side effect of adding to sensitivity in general. Internally the pregnant woman is going through quite enough irritation. Addition of irritation from the outside may cause such common reactions as previously acceptable smells or tastes resulting in nausea. Emotional communications that would normally have very moderate effects result in extreme reactions. What all this boils down to is that the mother's nervous system is becoming more and more like that of a newborn's—hypersensitive. This not only is good but is required to facilitate the mother-infant bond. The baby and mother can remain one and the same if her system is like the baby's. Fusion will be promoted. The importance of these phenomena cannot be overemphasized. They relate to the basic well-being of both mother and baby. They relate to reduced risks of either one developing cancer later in life.

Having one's first baby after the age of thirty is usually a life-style decision. But few experts choose to point out publicly that one of the highest risk categories for breast cancer is women who make this choice—delaying pregnancy while pursuing other goals first. If the genetic material of the ova becomes unstable with age, why should we assume that other cells in the body might not also become less stable with age. Unstable genetic material has been shown to relate to cancer. So here we have a woman whose breast tissues are being subjected to the irritating effects of hormones in the course of pregnancy. If she is eighteen, twenty-three, or even in her late twenties the hormones are irritating cells that have a greater chance of being genetically stable. Add hormones to unstable genetic structure and two to five or even eight years later another case is added to the statistics of breast cancer. Waiting to have a first pregnancy after age thirty is potentially dangerous to the mother. It seems clear that the hormonal onslaught of a first pregnancy is far more intensive than in subsequent pregnancies.

IF PREGNANCY DOES occur for the first time in a woman over thirty, her seeming maturity should not be allowed to stand in the way of her being babied by those who love her. Women at any age can best be protected from increased biochemical irritation through proper loving and comforting. The hormones are more than enough irritation. Their effects should be soothed as much as possible to prevent a chain of adrenaline-based reactions. The greater the sensitivity, the greater the potential for feelings triggering biochemical explosions.

The pregnant women most likely to have their nervous systems become hypersensitive and infantlike are paradoxically the most mature and emotionally stable. To become immature in the course of pregnancy requires great maturity. In order to discuss this, we need a clear concept of maturity. There are twenty year olds who seem to possess the wisdom and judgment of a wise old sage. And there are sixty-five year olds who have the emotional development of a toddler. Emotional maturity after adolescence does not seem to necessitate significant increase in chronological age. Years of experience can help create a sense of wisdom, of knowing. But without a solid emotional foundation, the experience of the years seems never to accumulate. There is nothing for it to build upon.

According to most psychological theories, to be mature means to be able to have and be comfortable with all of one's feelings. Some people use distance and/or tough guy tactics to avoid feelings. Intimacy is frightening to them. Some people will appear to be sugar-coated as a means of denying their anger. Nothing seems to bother them. They are avoiding their rage. Many studies point out that women who cannot express anger are more likely to get breast cancer. But extreme anger, on the other hand, can be used to push people away and is also carcinogenic. When any one feeling is dominant, whenever anyone has obsessions with powerful feelings attached to the thoughts, that person is out of balance. Having feelings that are too powerful and too chronic is not healthful. Whatever the prolonged or powerful feeling, it is going to have biochemical consequences. If it is worry, loneliness, or depression, the feelings correlate with cancer. Whenever feelings are too dominantly oriented in one direction they are immature. A mature person can have lots of feelings, has learned how to moderate these feelings, and basically seeks relief from feelings that are too much. Mature people do not stew in their own juices, they do not let anything eat them up alive or make mountains out of molehills.

One theory of maturity centers upon the idea that we should all be able to accept feeling inadequate and imperfect and assume that we can never really be the best at something. Supposedly this is to take performance anxiety pressure off people. The trouble is that it also seems to create feelings of despair and depression. Certainly we should be able to recognize when we have failed or been inadequate. But after that, attempting a different approach to solving the problem at least allows for the chance that the problem will get solved. If people really could accept being inadequate, no one would seek the services of a mental health professional. If people could accept being inadequate, they probably would give up easily on their problematic marriages. If people could accept being inadequate, they would simply give up and be depressed, feeling hopeless and helpless. Just think what happened to the American auto industry when the feeling was that Japan and Germany would always make better cars. An entire industry got emotionally depressed due to feeling inadequate. Once the need to be the best reemerged, the industry got a kick in the pants. Their products are much better today and are still getting better. There is nothing wrong with being inadequate. There is something very wrong with desiring to stay that way. There is nothing wrong with making mistakes.

There is something very wrong with repeating the same ones over and over.

In my opinion, giving up without doing everything reasonable first is a clear sign of immaturity. It happens in industry, in families, in marriages, and in individuals. Being hopeful and optimistic about finding a way out of problems is a mature means of dealing with depression.

Studies indicate that attitude and stress have nothing to do with curing or reversing cancers. What does matter is how a person processes irritation; alone or in a fusional relationship. Maintaining hope is important in at least improving the quality of life for a patient with a "hopeless" diagnosis. Fighting to the last minute does not save lives. What it does accomplish is to not force the patient to stare death in the face the whole time. And besides, there are case after case of "hopeless" cancers being survived and defeated. No cancer has to be viewed as utterly hopeless.

Cancer patients are extremists with feelings. They can be furiously angry, hopelessly depressed, and/or chronically worried. They process emotional and life event irritation in an isolated way. They do not use loved ones to lower their levels of angst. Instead they absorb everyone else's. In a clear sense, people who develop cancer are at least in some specific areas less mature than people who do not. The balance is not within them.

Maturity is just that, a balancing of feelings. Because of this, mature people can more easily keep things in perspective. Perspective is the key word. It requires that the individual process irritation by not blowing things out of proportion. It requires that the individual have a sense of priorities that puts love and relationships at the top of the list. Maintaining a perspective in life is anti-cancer. It is most easily accomplished when a team approach is used. You can help each other keep this all-important perspective. Mature people can be caring and also accept caring. This helps keep a perspective. Having the opportunity to share problems permits a married couple to have better chances of reaching a workable perspective. They can bounce things off each other in ways single people cannot.

A pregnant woman who is mature will use other people to help her feel safe. Her husband's caring gestures will be accepted. She will not see them as infantizing. She will see them as loving, and she will be comfortable with them. Her parents, sisters and brothers, in-laws and friends will be there to help reduce her anxiety. This will all contribute to a safer feeling and thus permit her to have her childlike immature feelings right along with her adult ones. But most important, an emotionally mature woman will not be overly frightened by the powerful feelings of infancy that are being rekindled in her. She knows, she can sense, that this is temporary, that she will leave these powerful feelings behind her after they serve their purpose. When her moods are extreme, she knows that someone is there to soothe her. This gives her license to be moody. Her hypersensitivity to smells and tastes will be joked about but also respected by her support system. Her emotional irritability may be more difficult to deal with, but it too will be accepted. She is safe to be herself.

The immature mother-to-be is also frightened. She cannot trust herself or her support systems. She is afraid that she might get in touch with very infantile feelings and not be able to give them up. The immature pregnant woman is afraid of going off the deep end. The reactions in her body are extremely frightening. She has lost control of what is happening and cannot trust others to care for her properly. She has no choice but to fight regression back to her own infancy. She will see loving, giving gestures as silly. She will work to maintain an air of maturity and stoicism that is the ultimate cover for her terror of pregnancy and childbirth. Being cared for is unsafe, particularly when she is so vulnerable. It brings her back to the negativity of her own actual infancy. It reawakens too much. She will not permit her nervous system to become optimally hyperirritated.

The mature woman's nervous system will paradoxically be

106

very infantile. Right after birth she will be a matched set with the nervous system of her baby. The bonding will be much more complete and intense. The immature woman will resist permitting her regression back to the level of a newborn baby. The bonding will thus have to be aberrant.

It is the husband's responsibility in pregnancy to do all he can to prevent any interference with the mother's future ability to bond with her newborn. His job will be to mother the mother-to-be. The more effectively he can do this job, the safer and more hospitable the environment for the developing baby. The more cared for and accepted she is in pregnancy, the more caring and accepting she will be for the newborn. Everything that transpires between the husband and the infantile aspects of his wife's nervous system is a test. It is a test of how safe she will be at childbirth, the most vulnerable position to be in for any adult human being.

The "pregnant" husband must recognize that his feelings are secondary to those of his pregnant wife's. He must take second place in all emotional matters. His hormones are not overwhelming him. And his systems, while more sensitive than usual, cannot compare to the sensitivity of his wife's. If she seems to be unreasonable and demanding, he must be determined to accept these primitive feelings in her. It is not easy. At times every man can easily fail. If one keeps in mind the idea that in many ways she is becoming a baby, the job is much easier. If he can see only the adult in her, he will fail.

A mature, properly regressing pregnant woman is much easier to care for. She will not be embarrassed to let her needs be known. She will seek closeness and physical affection. Sex will remain part of her life. She will recognize through her more adult emotional parts that even if she is no longer interested, her husband will need to be satisfied. Without this satisfaction many men withdraw. The husband then becomes a neglectful mother. So even in pregnancy, even with her feelings being more important, and even with her disinterest at times, she must help to keep him capable of remaining loving and giving.

The immature pregnant woman will also become more irritable. However, she will use irritability to push others away. This pushing away in pregnancy is a foreboding of the postpartem depression that frequently follows birth. Postpartem depression translates to an inability to fuse with the baby. The degree of depression varies, but it always means that the fusion with the newborn is not progressing as it should. It is the husband's job to prevent it. Forget the nonsense of hormone imbalance being the cause. If hormones were the explanation for postpartem depression, every woman would suffer from it. Again, it is *how* the woman processes the irritation during pregnancy that is important. Whether or not she is emotionally mature or immature is secondary to whether or not she has a husband who can get past her defenses to soothe and comfort her.

The husband must not fall for a pushing away tactic. Gentle but firm insistence is necessary. Words may be too irritating; a touch or smile may be enough. But the wife must not be allowed to withdraw into isolation in the course of the pregnancy. If she does show signs of regressing (hypersensitivity, mood swings, clinginess), she should be helped to be more comfortable with them. One young husband I know brought flowers and cutesy stuffed animals for his wife. She objected to the waste of money and seemed unappreciative, but he continued until they could joke about it and try to figure out which ones the baby would like. At times he also acted silly and childish. This granted the necessary permission for her to share in these feelings. She turned out to be a wonderful mother for her newborn. It is doubtful that she would have been if he had not helped her past her fear of being babylike.

If there was prepregnancy resentment toward the wife, the husband should try to suspend these feelings as much as possible. That may seem like an impossible suggestion, but if he realizes that he is also caring for his unborn child by caring for his wife he may more easily overcome any resentment he has for her. She is the medium through which to care for the developing baby. If it cannot be done for her, perhaps it can be done for this future offspring. The safety of the in utero baby is largely in the future daddy's hands.

He should make sure that she gets enough rest and do all he can to reduce her external stress. Financial problems should not be discussed at this time, nor should her inadequacies be pointed out to her. No irritation of any kind should be added to her preexisting irritation from pregnancy.

What all this amounts to is the husband should treat his wife as he would have her treat their baby. It is a practice run on early child rearing and the mom-to-be is the training doll.

Physical affection is as important now as it was when she was an infant. And care and extra tenderness are required. She feels fragile at times, and this must be respected. Her legs, back, abdomen, and other parts of her body may be more and more strained as pregnancy progresses. Gently massaging strained areas is a must. It provides the same touch that she will use to soothe the baby. Rub lotion on her stretching abdomen. Share the feelings of the baby's movement. Be insistent if she resists. But insist with sensitive humor or tenderness. Forcing someone to accept loving is like trying to force children to respect their parents. Certain things cannot be forced but require insistence and persistence instead.

No husband ever says, "Now I am going to contribute to my baby's and perhaps my wife's future cancer by not caring for them properly." But all husbands should know that we have data that indicate that aberrations of the mother-infant bond may very well contribute to future emotional and physical problems (cancer included) of the child. Husbands must understand that they have a very great responsibility to assist their unborn baby. They must take charge of caring for their wives.

CHERYL AND ADAM have been married for two years. They were very much in love when they decided to become pregnant. Being young and healthy, sex was frequent and enjoyable. They paid no attention to thermometers and the proper time of the month to conceive. They just did what they always did and did it as frequently as they always did. Within two months of deciding, Cheryl was pregnant.

Adam is a copilot for an air-freight company. Some day he hopes to fly for a major airline. When Cheryl got the test results back, she went to a toy store. She purchased two model 747s and a tiny single-engine model jet. They were waiting for him on the kitchen table when he came home. At first he did not catch on. After a moment it hit him. He went over and tenderly kissed her nose, eyes, then her lips. All he wanted to know was how she was feeling. Cheryl laughed at his mother hen concern and told him she was fine, that according to the doctor she was pregnant for only three weeks. They went for a walk after dinner, and he asked if it was safe to make love; they did, and then fell asleep entwined in each other.

During the next two months Cheryl got more and more tired and queasy. Adam started reading about pregnancy and found out that plain crackers help with morning sickness. He purchased every brand imaginable. When she was throwing up he was there rubbing her back. Adam's only concern was for her. They adjusted their social schedule to allow for more sleep.

Adam thought they should find out about genetic counseling. They spent eighty dollars and were told by the experts that they were an extremely low risk for any problems. He noticed a poster for a free prenatal nutrition course offered by the hospital. They attended, and Cheryl was happy to learn that she already was eating properly. By the fourth month the nausea stopped, but a craving for pizza began. Gino's Pizza Parlor could not have been more pleased. Adam had read that pizza, while highly caloric, is also highly nutritious. Several nights a week the kid from Gino's was at their door.

When she began to really show in the second trimester they both got even more excited if that was possible. At a routine doctor's visit he put a beltlike fetal monitoring device around her middle. Upon hearing the fetal heartbeat they both had tears in their eyes. To celebrate he took her shopping for maternity clothes. They joked about how expansive the stretch waistbands were. They purchased pink pajamas with a flap in the back. Adam was concerned about his weight being on top of little Amanda or little Jake during lovemaking. The back flap got a lot of use.

Cheryl was getting more and more excited but also frightened. Her fears centered upon losing control and childbirth. When she told Adam this he hit the books again. He believed that with information instead of ignorance he could be more reassuring. In reality, information was far too rational to soothe her feelings. His interest and love were what actually did the trick. She was appreciative of his interest, but more than that she felt his concern. His gentle voice made her feel relaxed and warm. She glowed from his touch, from his voice.

Smells bothered her seriously by the time the sixth month began. She was repulsed by certain foods. Hot dogs and other processed meats had long been her favorites, but now their smell and taste were intolerable. Her eyes were more irritated by her friends' cigarette smoking, and Cheryl had to be convinced that it was permissible to ask her friends to refrain from smoking in her presence. When one friend said she couldn't sit long without a cigarette, Cheryl gave her an ultimatum, "Look, you can smoke here, but I'll probably barf on your head. Go ahead, I don't mind."

The Lamaze training had been completed weeks before the baby was due, and they had met several nice young couples there. The teacher was a sweet, middle-aged nurse, who patiently answered all of the questions, sophisticated or naive. Cheryl and Adam practiced diligently at home. One week before her due date she started to experience a cramping feeling that she attributed to the Chinese food she had eaten for dinner. She thought the indigestion would go away if she went to the bathroom. The cramping feeling got more frequent and more powerful. She remembered that her Lamaze instructor had said that this may be a symptom of labor. Adam got a gentle shove, looked at the clock, complained that it was only four in the morning, then sprang out of bed like a Red Hawk missile and took her to the hospital.

In the labor room Adam coached her in proper breathing. Labor lasted four hours. The delivery progressed just as the instructor had described it. It ended with Amanda resting on her mother's stomach. The cord was literally cut, but figuratively, it could not be touched. Amanda was magnificent, weighing in at eight pounds, two ounces. They took her away to clean her up, and Cheryl almost got off the delivery table to follow. When Amanda returned to her mother's warmth she stopped crying. The nurses, obstetrician, and anesthesiologist (extra baggage in this case) were remarkably silent. For them too this birth was a deep emotional experience. They saw a couple and a baby in love. They saw the basic unit of survival for mankind. One nurse was crying. The anesthesiologist had a smile of total contentment. Seven people were witness to how it is supposed to be.

And then Adam almost passed out. His blood pressure dropped to seventy over forty. His legs turned to Jell-O. The room began to spin. One of the nurses noticed his condition and shoved a wheelchair under him. He was in a cold sweat, and his skin was clammy and translucent. He was the first to leave the delivery room. With his last bit of controllable strength he muttered something about not worrying her. A half hour resting and he was fine. He probably had his pressure checked more than Cheryl did. He felt better but embarrassed and he drifted off to sleep. He was moved to an unoccupied room, and within an hour the family was all asleep.

The next day he arrived with gifts for Cheryl and the baby. Cheryl got the gold bracelet she had admired at the mall. And Amanda got, well, an unusual gift. Adam had painted several tiny model airplanes, including the little jet Cheryl gave him, pink, yellow, and white. He had made a mobile out of them by joining two aluminum rods with monofilament. Cheryl loved the bracelet, but the mobile was so loving she was overwhelmed. She cried and pulled him to her. They both cried.

From before her beginnings Amanda was being emotionally educated to most likely suffer from fewer and less intense psychosomatic disorders. She was being set up to have a more efficient immune system. She was being set up to outlive longevity statistics. Some would credit all of this to heredity. After all, good health does seem to run in families. But so does caring, love, and involvement.

Amanda will someday be in a loving marriage much like her parents. She will expect that normal human relations are like her parents'. Any man who cannot love her as her mother, Cheryl, did will be viewed as strange, bizarre, just not right. The man she marries will care for her during pregnancy as her mother was cared for. Her children will then unconsciously seek mates who fit into this pattern.

Medical science, in its frustration at not being able to answer the questions raised by cancer, frequently falls back on the helpless and hopeless position of heredity. Cancer does run in families. But so does criminality, alcoholism, and schizophrenia. People also like to see these as hereditary. We can see how an anti-cancer position can be passed from Cheryl's link to Amanda and then to Amanda's children and so on.

Adam is the anti-cancer inoculation for both Cheryl and Amanda. It was not only the unsolicited gifts he brought her; equally important was his fascination with the whole process. By the time Amanda was there to look up at his face Adam could have taught a basic course on embryology or the physiology of pregnancy. He learned all this to allay his fears as much as Cheryl's. When he discussed all of this with Cheryl, she felt what was behind his concern—love.

Her moods were frequently extreme, and he accepted this. When he did, she somehow gave up the need to be weepy or "out to lunch" more easily. When on occasion he was not perfect, she was more likely to withdraw and remain buried in her irritated feelings. With few exceptions, however, he was close to totally accepting. This set the stage for Cheryl being almost totally accepting of Amanda. This was also setting the stage for a repetition of the entire process in the next generation.

If Cheryl had had other motives for having a baby besides sharing Amanda with Adam, if her desire had been to use Amanda for her own specific purposes, if Amanda had been supposed to prove Cheryl's adequacy as a woman, things would have been very different. It is not often that delivery room personnel shut up. It is even rarer for them to be moved to tears by a birth. They sensed something was unique about this young couple and baby. It's such a shame that it is that unique!

6

The Female Holocaust

THE 5:40 TO GREAT NECK was possible if he could hustle just a little bit faster through the Penn Station crowd. At 6′3″, Sid towered over people as he pushed ahead. As he rushed along, women turned to look. He was wearing a dark blue pinstripe by Yves Saint Laurent. His shirt was Jeffrey Banks, and his tie by Liberty of London. Italian cuts looked perfect on his 190-pound frame. He had light sandy-blond hair and blue eyes. The gold Rolex and alligator attaché were the finishing touches. He would be an ideal model to sell expensive watches, autos, or anything.

It was always the third car from the end where the evening poker game was held. After Harvey moved to Florida, Sid was asked to be the fourth. He is the youngest of them. Irv, the oldest, is a balding chubby man who cannot help but look sloppy. Regardless of the expense and care he goes to in selecting clothes and regardless of his success in the clothing business, Irv looks like the antithesis of Sid. Jack, who has graying temples and a penchant for Ralph Lauren suits, owns an accounting firm with offices in Manhattan and Boston. Making the 5:40 means it cannot be tax season. Tax season means a suspension of the game. Tax season means Jack does not see his Great Neck home for weeks on end.

Brian is only seven years older than Sid. He is in excellent physical condition and very concerned about it. His cholesterol is low, as are his triglicerides. His standing at the country club is high, however. He is the creative head of one of the nation's leading advertising firms.

All four could afford to commute by private limousine. Sid used to drive his 450 SEL into Manhattan each day, but an hour and fifteen minutes in rush-hour traffic was too much. The evening game and comradeship was much better than sitting in traffic.

All the men are well educated and well above the median income, not only for America, but even for Long Island, New York. They all are Jewish and are all married to Jewish women. Their wives are all statistically far more likely than any other women in the world to develop breast cancer.

Sid bounded up to the two facing, padded seats. Jack slid toward the window, no longer having to save the seat. Irv jokingly said, "Almost missed the train again. If you would just stop putting it to that gorgeous secretary of yours, you wouldn't have to rush to make the train everyday."

Jack, the accountant, snapped, "Shut up and deal. I'm in the hole for twelve bucks from yesterday. Phyllis threatened a divorce if I keep compulsively gambling away the family fortune. So how about joining me for the weekend in Atlantic City?"

Brian looked up. Something was bothering him, but he just smiled. Sid turned to him and asked, "Brian, my old pal, do you know how to get a Jewish nymphomaniac to stop having sex?" Before Brian could respond Jack and Irv said, "Marry her!"

Jokes about Jewish wives, hostile denigrating jokes about Jewish wives, continued for the entire trip to Great Neck. Every joke told spoke about sexual inadequacies or cruelty or sadism or perhaps how lazy and spoiled Jewish wives supposedly are.

Mostly they were sad attempts at comic commentaries on the supposed inability of Jewish wives to accept their husbands sexually.

They continued to laugh as each member of the foursome tried to outdo the others. None of them made any connection between their jokes and the more serious side of their life-styles. None of them connected their jokes to the local newspaper headlines that placed their community, Nassau County, New York, at the top of the statistical list for the incidence of breast cancer. Between the years 1976 and 1980, Nassau averaged 111.73 cases per 100,000 women. The national average for the same time period was 86 per 100,000. Neighboring areas were higher than the national average, but none compared with Nassau. And horribly enough, Nassau's death rate for breast cancer also took the top position, with 47.3 deaths per 100,000 women in 1982. This county in New York state has had a remarkably high incidence of breast cancer since almost immediately after World War II.

Although it seems to be stretching the limits of plausibility to connect Jewish wife jokes to breast cancer, I believe these jokes are indicative of the only reasonable explanation of this strange, high incidence of this terrifying disorder. Let me explain.

Recently the American Cancer Society admitted it was baffled by these statistics. None of the usual tie-ins of cancer rates and identifiable variables were there.

What we do know relates back to our 5:40 card game. The women most likely to develop breast cancer are married to or divorced from men such as these. They reside in Nassau. They are Jewish, and they also have had their first full-term pregnancy after the age of thirty. The women also have an early onset of menstruation and late menopause, resulting in longer exposure to hormonal factors. If they do not have their first full-term pregnancy after thirty, they are likely never to have a child. Ten percent excess body weight is common. They are of a high socioeconomic status. Estrogen replacement therapy is part of their coping with menopause. And some other female in the family will have had a history of breast cancer.

In January 1984, *Newsday,* the Long Island newspaper, published a Sunday feature titled, "Long Island's Cancer Mystery." The article pointed out only that "science" remains stumped by the statistics. The first photo, however, revealed the journalist's prejudice. It showed a middle-aged mother with a history of breast cancer and her adult daughter smiling sadly at the camera. Whenever established researchers cannot answer a question, heredity and, frequently, viruses are the cushion to fall back upon. The photo implied that heredity plays a part in breast cancer. I am convinced this is not true; here's why:

To begin with, medical science has found almost no cases of identical twins (monozygotic) developing the same kind of cancer. In fact, if one gets cancer, the other usually does not. These are people with the same exact genetic makeup. They have been exposed to the same nutrition, the same viruses, and the same carcinogens. But they have not been exposed to the same emotional environment. Frequently twins are inadvertently placed in good twin-bad twin categories right from the beginning of life. They process irritation differently based upon being placed in these roles. One may be more even-tempered, more comfortable with accepting of care from others. The other may be more anxious and more likely to be unable to fuse with others. Psychologists who have studied identical twins point out that superficially many traits are similar, but there are significant personality differences. These differences are learned right from the start.

Let us travel into Manhattan and compare the Jewish women of Long Island with their cousins, the Hassidic Jews. These are people who do not tell jokes about their wives. They do not complain about or discuss their personal sexual problems. They are orthodox in their religious views. The extended family still exists. Marriage and first pregnancy occur earlier in life. They do not believe in abortion or divorce. They eat horrendously fatty foods and work in high pressure businesses. But these women suffer far fewer cases of breast cancer than their cousins just twenty miles away.

Cancer—breast cancer also—is not hereditary. If a sister or mother had it, did she also have an unhappy marriage? Was she also more likely to absorb the emotional irritations of her husband and children? In other words, was she a stereotypic Jewish mother? Having poor marriages, even getting divorced does run in families, Jewish and non-Jewish. It is a learned response passed on from one generation to the next. Jews in Nassau County have a significantly higher divorce rate than most other Americans. In Nassau County, Christians also have a higher than average divorce rate.

Christian women living on Long Island do get breast cancer more frequently. But not as frequently as their Jewish neighbors. Whether the woman is Jewish or Christian, if she is in an unhappy marriage or if her marriage has ended, the risks are much greater.

Breast cancer, like almost all other cancer, has increased as the divorce rate increased after World War II. Breast cancer occurs far less frequently in areas of the world where divorce and adultery are infrequent. It occurs less frequently in Hassidic Jews and Masai Africans. They both eat fatty diets. It occurs less frequently in the Crimea and Caucasus Mountains of the Soviet Union where the inhabitants eat fatty foods and excessive amounts of red meat. But they do not get divorced. They live in extended families, and they live to old age. And they do not tell hostile jokes about their wives.

The British, however, do. In London, the longest-running comedy in the history of Great Britain is *No Sex Please, I'm British.* British humor frequently centers upon the same type of marital problems as Long Island Jews. British women suffer from a significantly high breast cancer rate. In Sweden, the high

119

divorce rate, high incidence of depression, and liberal sexual attitudes are well documented. According to Swedish experts, the extended family has greatly declined in recent years. The breast cancer rate is also significantly high.

In chapter 5, I discussed the biological reasons why having a delayed first full-term pregnancy is a factor for increased risk. But why is it that so many Long Island Jewish women are choosing to do just that—delay child rearing? Jews in America are probably no longer worried about survival. As the traditions of Judaism are shed for the American dream, major life-style changes are occurring. This is true for many people who have made America home. In Japan, women have a low incidence of breast cancer. When they move to America, it takes two generations before they are sufficiently Americanized to have a rate like most American women. Diet is not enough of an answer. Life-style is.

But for the Jews, the collective fears of the Diaspora have led to a unique coping mechanism. Charles Silberman, in his book *A Certain People: American Jews and Their Lives Today,* points out that: "In almost every field they have entered, be it crime or medicine, scientific research or real estate development, journalism or commodities trading, Jews have gravitated to the top." When striving to emulate the upper crust of Long Island's Christian community, Jews have sought similar status, security, and wealth.

In recent years anti-Semitism in America has been greatly reduced. While it is still present, it is not nearly as significant as it was a generation or two ago. In the 1960s, restrictions and quotas were done away with at the best universities and in many top corporations. At the same time the women's movement was pushing ahead. Doors were opened for women and Jews. It also meant they were opened for Jewish women. Many of the leaders of the civil rights and women's rights movements were Jewish.

The changes have been so rapid that Jewish women have had little time to evaluate the impact upon their life-styles. Bright, young, assertive Jewish women entered professions, business, and public service. They pursued medical, legal, and corporate careers. Marriage and babies were put on a back burner.

Life-styles are now totally different from the teachings of thousands of years. Youth and marriage are no longer seen as a good combination even though for centuries this was the case. As life-styles changed, so did the breast cancer rates. The Jewish women of Nassau County have evolved into the epitome of high need, achieving, successful American women. Until a balance is reached for American women between what they want and what they are willing to sacrifice, the breast cancer rate will remain high. If young, bright women living in the high pressure areas of our country can get a better perspective on life, perhaps their lives do not have to be so short.

When the breast cancer statistics were first published, scientists claimed that the higher incidence of breast cancer in Jewish women was due to the drinking water in Nassau County. Were we to believe that Catholic and Protestant women do not drink water? Were we to believe they drink only bottled water while affluent Jewish women drink from the tap?

Some think a contributing factor is overweight. Many Americans are overweight. The eating habits of this nation are at times absurd. But if we again listen to the "experts" as opposed to common sense, we get no real connections between nutrition, body weight, and cancer. At present the American Cancer Society and the National Cancer Institute are pointing out that fats and red meats are greatly contributing to cancer rates. Studies from California now indicate that vegetables and fruits are carcinogenic. Exercise has even been indicted as liberating free radical ions, a chemical imbalance seen by some to increase risks. The cardiologists tell us to eat fruits and vegetables and to exercise or we will die. The cancer nutrition experts are telling us to remain sedentary and eat rocks at this point! Let's examine this issue in terms of the diets of this high-risk group on Long Island.

More important than what is eaten is how we eat. Americans overeat. This is carcinogenic. The Long Island women who are 10 percent overweight are overeating. But more important than this obvious connection is the reason behind overeating. When people are depressed, overeating in general, and a sweet tooth specifically, is not at all uncommon. When people bond inadequately in marriage they will be depressed. When they gain excess weight they will be more likely to be less appealing and more likely to be self-conscious. So the weight can actually help in the pushing-away type of depression that has been correlated with cancer.

Which came first does not matter. Being fat and being sexy do not usually go together. It is a hostile act toward one's spouse to look unappealing. If one's spouse is telling hostile jokes about one's sexual inadequacies then weight gain is a means of expressing depression and anger. It does, however, amount to cutting off one's breast to spite one's vagina. Proper body weight is vital in preventing breast cancer and perhaps other cancer as well. It means the individual is not overtaxing the digestive system. It means the person is less likely to be depressed. It means the person is more likely to be happy with her body and thus more sexual and fusional in life.

Apparently the most purely physiological risk factor in breast cancer centers upon hormones. Previously I have pointed out the importance of hormones in growth, healing, and the evolution of cancer. An early age of menarche (menstruation) coupled with a late onset of menopause significantly increase the risks. Interestingly the statistics for cancer have almost always placed youth and old age as the greatest risk periods. In very young people the genetic material is constantly going through multiplication and division as the cells divide in the growth process. Youth is the time for rapid growth. Growth is a time for less stable genetic material. Couple this normal growth hormone level with a sudden increase in female hormones during the start of menstruation and the system can easily get jolted. When growth has somewhat slowed down in latter preadolescence and adolescence, the shock of increased female hormones is not as great. Early onset of menstruation also means that exposure to these hormones is for a longer time period during a lifetime.

Late menopause means the same thing, longer exposure to female hormones. But late menopause has other intrinsic risks. We have discussed the risk factors of late pregnancy, namely that with age genetic material is less stable. Cell division is not the culprit as in youth. The degenerative tissues of aging seem to be responsible. Whenever genetic material is less stable, the risk of cancer increases. Whenever hormone levels are prolonged or elevated, the risk of cancer increases. Infancy, pregnancy, adolescence, and sickness and injury all have certain elements of risk due to rapid cell division and elevated hormone levels. These times in life also have risks of triggering depressive reactions that again can correlate with malignancy.

With late menopause, hormones are remaining constant as the genetic material gets less stable with age. Menopause, at least in terms of cancer, can be viewed as natural protection against mixing together two potentially dangerous factors. The system was apparently established to maintain an internal biological balance. The balance is not there when menopause is late and genetic cell structures in different organ systems are less stable. Breast tissues get battered each month by female hormones. They will be a likely target site for the development of cancer.

When the natural process of menopause is interfered with by the use of estrogen therapies, another increase in cancer risk may occur, but there are sensible reasons for using estrogen. One of the most important is to help combat osteoporosis. Osteoporosis is a condition of mineral loss from bone tissue. It results in a gradual thinning and increased porosity of bones. Fractures and crippling can and do occur. It is the stooped over, old lady's disorder. It is a woman's issue because loss of bone occurs twice as fast as in men. Osteoporosis affects 25 percent of women after menopause. Surgical menopause (removal of the ovaries) without hormone replacement therapy results in a 50 percent chance of developing this condition. However, the severity of the disorder greatly varies.

Estrogen therapy prevents bone loss brought on by natural or artificial menopause. It is the most effective treatment to date. A low dosage must be started within three years of start of menopause to be most effective. Unlike breast tissue, bone tissue itself has no receptors for estrogen. The effects on bone are indirect and have to do with hormonal control of bone formation and breakdown.

Low dosage estrogen therapies are also used to treat less severe symptoms of menopause. Hot flashes, body hair growth, and mood swings are some of the most common. Natural estrogen decrease in menopause happens for very good physiological reasons. The cells with receptors for estrogen are less stable genetically at the age when the estrogen is reduced in the body. Medical science then gives the option to increase estrogen artificially in the body. The bad news is that the Nassau County women who are at greater risk of developing breast cancer have had early high-dosage estrogen therapy. Modern estrogen replacement therapy may be influential in reducing the risk, particularly when coupled with progesterone.

The truth is that we seem to be constantly changing our expert medical opinions about estrogen replacement therapy and hormones and cancer in general. Women should proceed cautiously in view of such a history of uncertainty. Please bear in mind that the people who said high-dosage mammography was safe are now saying that low-dosage mammography is safe. And the people who said high-dosage estrogen was safe are now saying low-dosage estrogen is safe. The absolute truth is that hormones cause greater instability and change in cell function and reproduction.

Pressure is on Long Island women, both from the outside and the inside. The need to achieve, to prove their capabilities, to be independent and assertive provide the outside pressures. These needs also increase anxiety reactions, result in chronic worry, and necessitate depressive and obsessive defenses. The results of all this are an increase in adrenaline-based reactions. Add hormones to the internal carcinogenic environment that adrenaline produces, and the inside pressures are obvious. Without means of dissipating these biochemical reactions, without means of moderating the external pressures, the risk of cancer is greatly increased. Fusional loving marriages help deal with both sides of this carcinogenic coin.

We can now see that delayed pregnancy, hormonal factors, excess body weight, and early estrogen therapy all have physiological effects. We can now see that they all can influence mood swings, increase sensitivity, and directly relate to depression— the kind related to cancer.

WHEN THE 5:40 pulled into Great Neck, the cards were put away. The four men started down the platform. Sid turned to Brian and asked if he needed a lift home. Brian explained that Cecilia was planning on meeting him and going out for dinner. He then added that his wife's way of calling the kids for dinner was "Get in the car." They all laughed. Sid responded with, "What does the average Jewish wife make for dinner anyway?" They all replied in unison, "Reservations." As they parted for their separate cars they called out their agreement to meet on the 5:40 the following night. But as they parted none of them reflected upon what these jokes might really mean. Were their wives too depressed to function? Was it their anger that caused them to reject sex? Did they get no joy out of caring for their children and husbands? Are their lives so pressured with their own business or professional requirements that cooking or caring for their families is a distant second place?

The foursome just laughed at these parting digs. They knew these jokes were originated by Jewish husbands so they did not think of them as anti-Semitic. It did not occur to them that Jews are the only ethnic group in America so furious with their wives and so dissatisfied with their marriages to tell such jokes. There are no Irish wife jokes, WASP wife jokes, Black wife jokes. There are only Jewish *wife* jokes.

Sid walked over to his Mercedes. The car responded with German discipline. It would not dare to hesitate to start. He pulled up to his garage and tapped the button to open the electric door. As always, the mail was waiting on the burled redwood dining room table. At the bottom of the bills and junk mail was an unaddressed manila envelope. He undid the metal tabs. His breathing stopped. His head pounded and he felt faint. He took the envelope and its contents over to the tufted leather couch in the living room. He opened his tie and collar button. With head in hands he read the letter from his wife, Marsha. It explained that the detective agency had taken the pictures. Marsha had taken the boys out that evening and was heading up to their condominium in Vermont. The boys wanted to know why Daddy was not coming and she said Daddy was too busy for them or for her. The letter went on, "I know you never really loved me. My father even told me that marrying a man like you, a man so into himself, so impressed with his looks and intelligence would be a big mistake. He was right, Sid. I did love you. I probably still do, but you killed us, you killed me. In Paris, in Cancun, in Copenhagen, even in the Catskills I saw you looking. At first I thought they were only looking at you. Then I saw how you looked back. Didn't you know what that did to me? How you tortured me? Sid, you're such an insecure, immature son of a bitch. Our honeymoon ended on our honeymoon. You were looking them over even then. I should have ended it when I first noticed. But I thought you were only looking.

These pictures show how wrong I can be. It's no wonder you kept me out of your office. When did you hire her? How long have the two of you been doing it? The strange part is I know there were others before her. I just kept lying to myself. Then I started to blame myself. I thought I was not pretty enough, or sexy enough for you. Well, Sidney, I'm pretty enough for a lot of men, and I'm going to find them. I like sex, Sid, just not with you.

"You gave me everything I ever wanted—except you. You were not there for me ever. You're no different than a lot of men in town. They're so impressed with themselves. I bet you all figure that it's the wives' fault. I bet you all think there are gorgeous women just waiting for you. That may be true. But it's true because they do not know you well enough. Once your young chippie gets to know you, she'll walk out on you too.

"Sidney, you are a fool. Like all the others around here, you have no idea what is going on. Wives are having affairs with delivery boys, finding lovers out in the Hamptons. They have no passion for husbands who are more interested in money and status seeking than their wives and families. Sidney, you've been married to the New York Stock Exchange, not me. You don't even know what you missed with your sons or with me. You missed the best time of their growing up. They don't really know you. You haven't been a father or a husband.

"When I get home on Sunday I want you out. I have sent copies of the photos to my attorney. I believe we can arrange the finances amicably. I gave up a good job in public relations with that publishing firm. I did it at the age of thirty-one to have your babies. I gave up a lot for you and now you owe me. But I want to be fair. I think we can settle out of court. For now, my dear Sidney, just get out of my home. You tortured me for years. You kept me worrying and jealous for years. I really enjoy hating you right now. I look at the pictures, Sidney, and I hate you. You cheated on me, but you also cheated on your sons. Don't try to talk me out of the divorce. You'll be hearing from my attorney."

127

He collapsed into the couch. He looked at his secretary having oral sex with him. He looked at the two of them having intercourse. He felt his world was falling apart. But he also felt worried that Marsha would get too much of his 2.3-million-dollar holdings. He was concerned about moving his clothing and other belongings temporarily to his firm's apartment in Manhattan. He was concerned about the boys. He was concerned about how hurt and angry Marsha seemed to be. He was concerned about what she could do. But he was most concerned about getting aroused by looking at the detective's photos. He felt his mind spin as he tried to somehow reconcile being so sexually excited as he pictured his children and wife disappearing from his life. His mind's eye rapidly switched back and forth from his secretary worshiping his phallus to any one who really mattered in his life hating him. He suddenly and violently vomited on his tufted leather couch, Persian rug, and dark blue pinstripe. He cried and then regained a little composure. He called his secretary.

Three years later Marsha was vomiting regularly and also suffering from diarrhea from chemotherapy. The surgeon who performed her mastectomy had recommended chemotherapy after so many lymph nodes were found to be malignant. She had gained almost twelve pounds after the divorce. She lost almost thirty pounds after surgery and chemo.

Since Marsha had first felt the lump in her right breast she had been through the medical wringer. Since Marsha had first suspected Sid of adultery and since the divorce, she had been through an emotional wringer. Worry and jealousy translate to elevated adrenaline-based reactions. These reactions place a person in grave danger.

Marsha had never in her entire life experienced a fusional relationship, not with her mother (a mother who, by the way, died from breast cancer) and not with her husband. The consequences of the lack of such a relationship are an elevated level of internal carcinogens.

128

After the divorce, Marsha tried like the Marines to find a few good men. She went out on many dates. Then there was Marty. He was good-looking but not like Sid. Marty was average height with curly dark hair. He was divorced also. He was frequently in Europe and Asia on business, but he shared interests with Marsha that Sid never had. Concerts at Lincoln Center, the art galleries and museums of Manhattan, the Mohonk Mountain House were their romantic haunts. The first summer after they met he took her to Europe. Walking to a train in France, he refused to help her carry her luggage. She had to chase after him dragging her bags. She became suspicious of him after this abuse, but she continued to date him. She decided one night to surprise him at his apartment. The housekeeper was willing to watch the boys, so she drove into the city.

Marsha bribed the super to let her into his apartment. She got undressed and climbed into bed to wait for him. After Sid, she found that she was capable of really enjoying sex. Marty was good, and she was excited waiting for him. By midnight he had not shown up, and she fell asleep. At one A.M. she awoke to noises in the living room. She got up to investigate. Marty and his neighbor, a tall willowy blonde, were kissing on the sofa. Marsha decided to end it, but to end it in style. Getting back in bed, she felt crushed for the second time in her life. She waited for them to come into the bedroom. They were totally naked. She sprang out of bed with just panties on and screamed, "Surprise." The two of them froze. She laughed and cried as she made her exit. He just stood there, naked in more than one way. This relationship died, just as her marriage had. One year later she was throwing up from chemotherapy.

She had been depressed since childhood, but until her marriage she did not connect her need to be alone, her mood swings, and her spaciness with being depressed. Her dating after her divorce awakened her to her depression. She was always at least mildly anxious, and she found she could only relate to men who were depressed and mildly anxious. She needed her mirror image to feel any comfort. Marty seemed to be made to order. He was not only anxious and depressed at times, but he had obvious mood swings and was quite capable of spacing out.

After five months of medical treatment Marsha entered entropic analysis (see *The Causes and Prevention of Cancer*). Her oncologist (cancer specialist) made the referral. His feeling was that medical procedures were not working, so as long as these psychotherapeutic techniques could not hurt, why not give it a try? He let it be known that he did not think she had much of a chance and this new analytic treatment would most likely just help her cope. As of this writing that was almost three years ago. Marsha has amazed everyone. Her hair has grown back, her weight is up, her white blood cells are at a high average level. All clinical means of detecting cancer show that she is apparently cancer free.

She still sees her analyst twice a week and checks in by phone every night of the year. Marsha feels she must find a man like her analyst in order to survive. This man would have to be capable of bonding, of enjoying her, and of great loyalty. Through her treatment she is experiencing this type of relationship for the first time in her life. Her oncologist keeps trying to refer more patients. Her analyst has no more available time for another patient. Training others in these techniques is what takes precedence for now.

By the way, Sidney married his secretary even though she is fifteen years his junior. They now have a young son. She is concerned about how hard and late he works. She is also concerned that a prettier, sexier secretary, stock broker, or whoever will throw herself at him. After all, that is what she did, and history does repeat itself. Perhaps she would be wise to find out the names of Marsha's doctors and analyst. Maybe she should keep them on file.

AFTER I APPEARED on a local Long Island television show discussing breast cancer, a woman from Nassau County called. She explained that she had lived all her life on Long Island and that with the exception of her, no one in her family ever had breast cancer. She said that her mother was a nutritionist and that she had followed an anti-cancer diet all her life. She never smoked or drank. She jogged over three miles of hills every morning. As she passed thirty-five, she was able to keep her weight down. Her children were all born before she was thirty. She concluded her description of why she should not have gotten breast cancer by stating, "I'm not even Jewish." Figuring I had nothing to lose, I asked, "When did you find out about him?" If this was irrelevant, I thought, that was vague enough for her to say, "What do you mean?" Instead she said with genuine amazement, "I found out two years ago and got separated and divorced almost immediately! How did you know?"

I hope by now the importance of fusional marriage can be appreciated. I hope the reader has an understanding of how aberrations of this fusion affect the body's chemistry in a carcinogenic way. Any one or all of the high-risk factors may or may not be present, i.e., being Jewish, delayed pregnancy, early menstruation, late menopause, and family history. What is always present is an inability to fuse, an inability to be cared for, an inability to relinquish control, to let go.

Marriage and sexuality provide the opportunity to repeat from infancy what was wonderful or horrendous. When divorce, adultery, or just a lack of involvement occur, the worst of early infancy gets repeated. Breast cancer all too often follows.

There are many marriages in which the wife cannot feel fusion regardless of how the husband behaves. He may make every reasonable attempt to get past her barriers. If the involvement is not there, if a connection is not there, the risks are. Women having these reactions report feeling crazy for not appreciating these "really nice" guys. They are totally confused as they transfer early infantile feelings onto a husband who perhaps does not deserve them. Regardless of the reason, if there is a powerful feeling that the marriage is just not right the risks will increase. If she cannot love him in spite of how giving he can be, the risks will increase. And if she starts acting against the marriage, the risks also increase.

LINDA IS A forty-six-year-old physician. She is very happily married—this time. Her first marriage also should have made her very happy. Chet was a warm, giving man. He was totally devoted to her and their daughter. He owned a chain of card shops throughout the Long Island area. The money came in, he did very little work, and their marriage went from not great to worse.

Linda was working long and hard at a large university hospital. She took time off from her residency to have her baby and returned to almost full-time work within five weeks. The baby was left to the care of a competent, sweet mother's helper from Utah. Linda liked the idea that this young Mormon girl was a very moral person who also did not smoke or drink.

Linda was constantly concerned about her daughter. She was even more concerned about not loving Chet. She could not accept the fact that she could not adequately connect to her child or her husband. He did everything right, and still she could not feel passion, desire, or almost anything for him. She told friends that she felt crazy, that something was very wrong with her not to be happy with him. She flirted with male colleagues but did nothing else.

Chet was obstinate about his need to be romantic. He frequently brought home flowers, took her to candlelight dinners, and loved to walk on the beach at night. Linda enjoyed all of these things, just not with him. She had married him because it made sense. He was going to be wealthy by inheriting the family business. He was wonderfully kind and generous. He was a gentle, considerate lover. He was just not right, but her rational mind said she was being foolish to pass up a man so devoted to her.

This is a frequent symptom of the infantile or pushing-away depression in both sexes. Everything is right, they function well together. But the blending, the fusion, the bond is not there. The partner who is dissatisfied is likely to feel crazy, to experience great guilt, and to suffer from mood swings and powerful intermittent depression. Extramarital sex is not uncommon in this day and age for either sex. When asked why they have affairs, they give the excuse of boredom or needing something that they could not identify that was just not there. Even if adultery is not part of it, not being able to love the spouse who is in love with them results in enormous guilt. This is all because of the infantile inability to fuse.

After six years of total discontent, Linda developed breast cancer. Chet had seen her through her surgery and radiotherapy. He had always been there for her. But somehow she knew the cancer was directly connected to her inability to be happy in this superficially perfect marriage. Painfully she explained all this to Chet. He was not in the least shocked. He was not surprised. He knew that somehow they were always out of sync. Perhaps he blamed himself. He refused to go along with the idea that her cancer was connected, however. They parted as friends.

Three years later Linda married another physician. He is a hard driving, somewhat egocentric man, the antithesis of Chet. Linda is happy now, but she is still plagued by the unanswered questions of her shattered first marriage. She explains. "I got breast cancer to get out of my first marriage. I guess I couldn't have unless something drastic could be blamed on that marriage. I really cannot complain about Chet at all. He's a wonderful guy. I never had any malice toward him or, for that matter, he toward me. It simply did not work for us.

"I know now, at least I strongly believe, I will have no reoccurrence of my carcinoma. It has served its purpose. The cost of my divorce was the emotional torture of going through a lumpectomy and radiotherapy. There is nothing scientific about what I am saying. But every time I discuss it with colleagues, even oncologists, none of them speak of it as ridiculous or absurd. Maybe they are humoring me, but I don't think so. Maybe they consider my ideas because I am a physician. Maybe they wouldn't if I was just a housewife. But I know I am right. I used cancer to end a marriage that was driving me crazy. I'm not afraid of it anymore. It has served its purpose."

Linda is not only an excellent doctor, but she is a very intuitive human being. I believe she is correct about her cancer. However, she still has difficulty bonding and is thus still at risk, regardless of her belief. But she does seem far happier in her present marriage. Her new husband is not nearly as warm and loving as Chet, and somehow this is more acceptable to her. Perhaps what drove her crazy in her first marriage was her inability to bond, even to such a caring person as Chet. Her husband now is somewhat distant. This takes the pressure off. She still needs this distance. This is how she started her life. It is what is familiar and thus comfortable.

Linda's daughter is already showing signs of avoiding intimacy. She is anxious and is constantly performing in an attempt to please her mother, to somehow be acceptable, to some day finally really have a mother. This little girl will more than likely follow in her mother's footsteps. She too will be a breast cancer risk.

AT THE TIME of this writing a major, heavily financed study is being conducted by the American Cancer Society and a local Long Island University. If they ask the right questions they will notice that breast cancer correlates with high G.N.P. and high real estate taxes, in other words life-style. And when they break down the elements of life-style, they will find that marriage is the most important factor.

7

The Real Agony and the Real Ecstasy—Child Rearing

TEDDY IS ALMOST TWO. He is one of those stocky little towheads destined to have hair that will match his big brown eyes. With his button nose and chubby cheeks, he could be a child model. Along with these entrancing good looks goes an entrancing personality. Teddy has had an extremely fusional relationship with his mom. He is very fortunate that his father is deeply in love with his mother. Throughout his pre-birth existence both of them took good care of him, his dad by showing understanding and love for his mom and his mom by feeling that Teddy and she were the same being. After birth unconditional love followed, with mom taking on the bulk of the child-care responsibilities. Dad was there to help, but admittedly could not calm down Teddy's upsets as easily as his wife. Dad also recognized that he could not relate to "a little beastie who just eats, sleeps, and dumps." Therein lies the hint of future problems that perhaps might have been avoided. If Teddy's mom had been more aware she might have been able to help her husband with the apparent animosity he would later feel toward his son.

Many men do not relate well to infants until they can offer a response to the stimuli the father provides. Fathers seem to need more clear responses from a baby in order to connect. Teddy's father did not appreciate or even understand the development of his newborn son. He never noticed which colors his son seemed to react to more powerfully. He never noticed how his new baby sneezed in bright light nor would he have questioned this phenomenon if he had noticed. He did comment once to his wife on how the baby reacted by splaying his arms and legs outward at the sudden sound of a balloon popping.

Now Teddy is almost two, and his father still does not understand anything about early childhood development. The truth is that John, his father, will probably not relate adequately to his son until the boy can learn to catch a ball. John played football in high school and continues to bask in the macho glory of victorious days. John is a very typical American dad. He loves his son but is afraid to mommy-coddle. The boy is not even two, and his father is afraid of being too affectionate, too soft. Real men throw around the pigskin, real men even throw hand grenades, if necessary, or pull lanyards on howitzers.

But by today's standards, it's all right for real men to heat a bottle, change a diaper, and cook a meal. When mother is working or overwhelmed by child-care responsibilities, real men can step in and help. Macho men who stay lost in the glory of football victories and military decorations rarely seem aware of their children's stages of development. If they ever do learn, all too often it is after the damage has been done.

John works hard as a management consultant. He is an expert at telling others what they are doing wrong and how to do it better, but he can accept no corrections of his own errors in relating to Teddy. At 7 P.M. on weekday nights dinner is served. Regardless of how tired or cranky he might be, Teddy must stay in his high chair until his dad has finished eating. John considers this to be proper etiquette, and you cannot start teaching proper etiquette too soon. Teddy's need to discharge internal irritation through movement, his need to simply blow off some steam is not appreciated. The fact that children under the age of two rarely have the attention span necessary to sit still under such circumstances is irrelevant, actually not even considered by John. After obvious discomfort levels are reached, Cindy, Teddy's mom, objects. John defends his position by pointing out all the poorly behaved children they both know. He admonishes that without firm controls and an appreciation for other's feelings, Teddy will grow to be another five- or six-year-old monster.

Yes, Cindy points out that Teddy is not even two. Yes, she points out that he will learn faster and more easily when he understands more. Yes, on several occasions she has simply taken Teddy away from the table. No, it has not changed John's attitude or beliefs one tiny bit. The conflict is beginning to end, however.

Teddy is taking responsibility. He is learning how to hold his tears in, how to sit quietly while his adrenal juices are overflowing, and how to feel that peace in his social world is solely up to him. He has already learned that daddy is loving, but also somehow dangerous. He will probably always be able to relate to male friends, but forever be afraid of really loving them.

All of this is happening simply because of John's lack of interest in and information about human development. Years from now Teddy will come to mom when John and he lock horns. It is a safe bet that Cindy will be in the bind of absorbing both of their emotional irritations. Eventually she will realize that she does not know whether her husband or son is the less mature. For years to come the marriage will have a major area of conflict, the raising of Teddy.

The more inadequate John feels, the more tenaciously he will cling to his ignorant position. The less Cindy is willing to sacrifice her son, the more conflict will ensue and the less fusional the marriage will become. Teddy is the guiltless cause of this negativity. This was a good pre-child marriage.

The presence of a youngster stimulates many feelings that

bring people back to their own early experience. Until he was old enough to wear shoulder pads, John was not really related to by his father. Being tough, being disciplined became the way to deal with other males. This is how John views his world. His mother feared his father. She sacrificed John. Their marriage was one of female subservience. John's mother died when he was seventeen. The cause of death was metastatic cervical cancer. The fate of this next generation remains to be seen. But Cindy is being placed at high risk.

FOR A GYMNAST, Susan's body is a bit chunky. She moves with a feline grace acquired only through years of diligent practice. Her French is also steadily improving. It is almost a second language to her. Again it indicates years of practice. Two weekday afternoons are for gymnastic workouts. Wednesdays are for French tutoring. The other two days are for a computer science course and for ballet. The ballet lessons would help the gymnastics along. The computer course was more obvious. After college anyone with a firm knowledge of computers would have a distinct advantage in this highly competitive world. The only problem is that Susan will have to wait as college will not begin for another thirteen or fourteen years. Susan is four years old.

While in utero, Susan's mother, Merle, read to her. She repeatedly went up and down pages of simple mathematics. And part of the reading was in French. Merle is convinced that the earlier children are exposed to the basics of education the faster they will learn. Faster is the key word. Merle has always been a performance anxiety baby herself. On a thin gold chain hangs her Phi Beta Kappa key. College at one of the Seven Sisters was just another area for her to excel. Tennis was her game but she realized that little Susan would not be able to handle even a lightweight graphite racket for several years to come. Gymnastics is perfect even for her chunky little daughter. Ballet also requires no adult strength. French and computers are where it is going to be. And Susan is going to have the edge. Merle has recently been attending Board of Education meetings to advocate all-day kindergarten. If this is not passed, she will probably send Susan to a private school. Time simply cannot be wasted.

Merle's marriage came as a result of not wanting to have an abortion. She had planned on marrying Evan anyway. The pregnancy just sped things up a bit. Merle finished her senior year both married and pregnant. She enjoyed it. She was moving ahead with her life faster than anyone else she knew.

While pregnant she studied everything she could about the best, the proper environment for her developing baby. Not only did she do the right things, she was obsessed about doing them. Susan was born to prove something about Merle's adequacy. Having a delightful, bright daughter was simply not enough.

Evan quickly caught on. At first he thought Merle's French lesson to a developing fetus was some sort of a joke, but after the arithmetic and beginning reading he realized she was not kidding. He at first attacked, pointing out that children who do learn to talk more slowly than average almost always catch up to their peers at some later date. They may even surpass many early speakers in terms of verbal abilities. He pointed out that boys develop more slowly than girls in almost all intellectual regards and that by the time they are preteens or certainly in early adolescence things equalize.

Evan thought he made a good case for not rushing education. What he did not consider was Merle's need to have not just a successful happy child, but rather a superkid. Like her mother, she would always be on top. Almost perfect means imperfect.

Evan soon realized that he was working against his wife's goals. When he and Suzie, as he called her, were alone, he strove for calm, low pressure activities, and just having fun. What really hurt him was Suzie's rejection. She had already fused to a woman dedicated to the ideals of the wunderkind. Calm and fun were foreign to her. Evan's desire for a Suzie was abandoned when he realized his daughter was definitely a Susan.

The powerful, maternal influence will almost always win out. Women should appreciate this tremendous power and use it cautiously.

Evan grew increasingly distant from both of them. Susan was Merle's life now. Through her she would accomplish great deeds. When Susan was three, Merle suggested they have another child. Evan vehemently objected. He feared more troops would be added to the enemy force. He did not trust Merle's use of the diaphragm, remembering Susan's "accidental" conception. He took over responsibility for birth control. Merle objected strongly to the use of condoms, and sexual contact diminished greatly.

Evan got the clear message that he was extra baggage. Had he gotten involved with the in utero speed-reading course, had he been thrilled by structured gymnastics as opposed to play-grounds, and had he any interest in college studies for toddlers, he might have been included, but Merle could not have permitted anything but agreement.

IN BOTH OF these cases, little Teddy and Susan, their births brought reawakened, powerful, early feelings for their parents. When one parent becomes convinced he is correct about some important issue and the other has the opposite view, compromises are rare because feelings are so primitive and powerful. Sides are drawn with one parent, usually the father, as the odd man out. Under such circumstances, the father may wind up emotionally bumped off. Mother and child are the new dyad to replace the emotional investment of the marriage. Regardless of whose judgment is wrong, the child will most typically gravitate to her. The opposite certainly does happen, but less frequently.

If the marriage was a good one prior to the birth of a child, compromises are usually easier to arrive at. If the marriage was not good, right or wrong conflicts will predominate. Teddy's mom could have entertained and distracted her son while daddy got his way at the dinner table. Instead it became a power play. Evan could have become an infiltrator into Merle and Susan's camp. Even if he totally disagreed, he would have had a chance of effecting some change. Withdrawing is surrendering the child.

To prevent most of these problems, parents need to have a knowledge of the normal range of developmental capacities of the child. If when to toilet train is not known, knowing how will not matter. And if the importance of the impressionability of the newborn is not appreciated the risk for damage is there. And when a child interferes with the capacity for love between the parents, something was very wrong before the child's birth. No child can be raised satisfactorily unless the parents are in a loving marriage. If the marriage is loveless the risks for the emotional annihilation of one parent will always be present as well as the likelihood of future observable psychological problems for the child.

A child develops into a representation of the marriage. If the marriage is warm and loving, the child will be warm and loving. Any chronic deviations from a fusional marriage will result in problems for the child.

Sometimes the child is used as a buffer to hold together a troubled marriage, but if there is a lack of love in the marriage, the child will feel unloved. If one partner is not showing attention to the other, the child will probably seek attention through any means available. If the parents are angry with each other, the child will very likely be angry. If the parents are prone to push each other away, the child will be depressed. Unhappiness in marriage translates into unhappy children.

Child abuse, whether it be violent or sexual, is always unhappy. It cannot happen when a marriage is good. If one parent is afraid of the other, that parent will not protect the offspring from whatever abuse the other may dole out. Fear and a desire to

141

maintain the marriage keeps her, or him, from intervening to stop the abuse. When sexual abuse occurs, the parent who is not the guilty one frequently finds it hard to believe.

Abused children who enter treatment usually report a genuine hatred for one of the parents in particular. It is almost a certainty that they will blame the parent who did not directly abuse them. The perpetrator of the deed becomes relatively unimportant. The parent who allowed the abuse to happen is seen as a collaborator. After World War II, men and women who collaborated with the Nazis or other Fascists were subjected to brutal retaliation from their countrymen. The people who pulled the trigger were hated, but with far less intensity than those who may have aided in the capture of hostages or resistance fighters. Nothing is worse than a collaborator. In severe child abuse situations, the ultimate choice, ending the marriage, may have to happen. If the nonabusive parent cannot effectively stop the abuse, no other choice remains.

Most people are not overtly abusive to children or spouses. Most abuse is far more subtle. When a woman or man attempts to destroy a child as a way of attacking the spouse, we have the child being used as a weapon. The destructive behavior may be obvious or it may just simply be a painful ignoring. Not speaking to or paying attention to a child is a quiet type of emotional homicide.

IN HER FRUSTRATION with her marriage, Lee has evolved into an emotionally abusive mother. Her husband, Brett, is away on business a great deal of the time. Even when he is home he is not really involved with his wife. He does, however, coach the Peter's Plumbing little league team. His nine-year-old son, Seth, is the pitcher. There is also three-year-old daughter, Caroline, who is daddy's little girl. He is affectionate and caring to his children. He is the opposite toward his wife. Tolerance is about all he feels toward her. She knows this.

When Brett is away on business, Lee seems unable to love or

even care for her children. Everything they do is an irritation. She becomes a harsh disciplinarian and shows no warmth even if they are sick or injured. When Brett is home she is frequently worse. She suffers whenever she watches him cuddling his children or whenever he teaches Seth a new pitch. Brett is using the children as weapons against her too. She is jealous of her children. Like Medea, she is attempting to destroy them emotionally in retaliation.

To end this problem would require the resolution of the block Brett has to loving his wife. Without love in this marriage, the children will continue to be used as weapons. With love, this deadly situation would most likely instantly disappear. Love could turn Medea into Mary Poppins.

The use of children as a buffer or weapon is a symptom of a carcinogenic marriage. When children are an enhancement to a marriage, the marriage is almost always anti-cancer.

Couples planning on having children often question their ability to be good parents. They wonder how anyone can put up with the crying, screaming, diapers, and feedings. What the young couple may not be taking into account is the feeling of having a baby belong to them. If it is conceived out of love, the baby will be part of both parents. Cleaning this baby, feeding this baby, and soothing this baby are equivalent to caring for one's self.

In a marriage, family, clan, tribe, or nation, belonging cannot be overemphasized. Right from the beginning of life, belonging is vital to human survival. The sense of security belonging provides protects the individual from the irritants from the outside and the inside as well. Sharing anxieties helps dissipate them. When a common threat exists, people rally to support each other. Belonging to the group offers safety.

Obviously the baby's belonging to her parents is required for survival. Later in life the sense of identity derived from belonging provides security that can lower internal carcinogen levels. Fear increases adrenaline, safety decreases it. Belonging to a spouse is almost as intense a sense of belonging as that between a mother and baby. Siblings and the extended family should follow in importance. Friendship also requires belonging. The more intense, the more a feeling of belonging. The lack of a sense of belonging is part of the cause of the depression so rampant today in Americans.

A generation or two ago, children typically were raised in extended families. Cousins were sometimes almost as close as siblings. Aunts and uncles filled in as surrogate parents. And grandma and grandpa were sometimes better than parents. They kept their children, the parents, from losing control when five year olds were being five year olds and sixteen year olds were being sixteen year olds. But the most important benefit derived from belonging to an extended family was the support young mothers received. When the newborn was overwhelming her she was not asked, she was told to take a break. Grandma or an aunt was there to step in before the mother would add irritation to an already irritated infant. The internal irritants would not have to reach dangerous levels for either the mother or infant. Genetic shifts in the baby's rapidly dividing cells would be less likely to occur. And for generations cancer remained far below the epidemic levels we see in today's American society.

The extended family is no longer nearly as frequent a life-style. A brother works in New York, a sister lives in California, and the grandparents have retired to Florida or Arizona. American mothers, since the social disruption of World War II, have been raising their babies in a greater degree of isolation than ever before. The cancer epidemic corresponds to this time of isolation.

Study after study demonstrates that women who raise children without support from other adults are far more likely to be child abusers. Belonging is necessary as a means of protecting infants. If the family is no longer present, we must have neighbors and friends pitching in as much as possible. No pregnant woman or new mother should be allowed to remain outside of social contact. If we permit this we are guilty of child abuse. If a neighbor is pregnant or has young children, get involved. Intrude, if necessary. It may be the only way past her depressive dynamics. If America can switch from the "me" generation back to the "we" generation, I believe we can reach cancer rates similar to pre-World War II. If not, we will watch helplessly as a third of our nation succumbs.

In areas of the world where the extended family still exists, cancer is a rarity. As soon as "progress" reaches these nations, tobacco and alcohol consumption increases. But more important, the family and the extended family begin to crumble. And when the extended family begins to crumble, the organ systems of the individual begin to crumble cancerously.

There is nothing new to these ideas. They are how mankind has survived and achieved for eons. Have we produced a Beethoven, Bach, Mozart, or Vivaldi since the Industrial Revolution? Has there been any architectural achievement to rival those of the generations of artisans and sculptors who built Versailles, the Cathedral at Reims, or Saint Peter's Basilica? Since the Industrial Revolution we have built bigger, but have we built better? Was there a different feeling in people, a purpose that belonging provided that does not exist once we get concerned with high Gross National Product? A sculptor at Reims taught his son to be a sculptor at Reims. The work passed from the hands of father to son.

Yes, this may have been horribly restrictive. And yes, it eliminated women from creative endeavors. I am not advocating this type of social order. I am suggesting that this type of belonging and the security it provided may have permitted a "Fifth Symphony," "the Brandenberg Concertos," or "The Four Seasons." It does not seem to be happening in our time. It is harder for us to belong. America grew out of the Industrial Revolution. As a nation we lack the depth, the antiquity of Europe, Africa, or Asia. We must therefore work harder and more deliberately at reestablishing the phenomenon of belonging. The social environment that produces enough security to create great art and to not create malignancies requires belonging.

When children reach post-toddler stage, they are old enough to begin identifying. Girls want to be like Mommy and boys emulate Daddy. This is a natural phenomenon unless one parent is so detached, hostile, or simply absent that only one parent is acceptable as a role model. Identification is a clear statement of the human being's need to belong. At these tender stages, mother and father identification is most important. But family, religious, ethnic, and national identification can also begin at this stage. Children should know of their heritage and familial or tribal traditions. Holidays should be observed and history should be taught. Begin the process with family, but add the Italian feast, the Irish Feis, the German oktoberfest, etc. Teach them of the accomplishments of your Hindu, Moslem, Jewish, Christian, or Shinto heritage. Children seem to thrive in such culturally rich surroundings.

Even if you have no sense of religion or group membership, do not deprive your child of the opportunity to make his or her own choice when old enough. And exposing yourself to customs and beliefs of your own background may be a new and very beneficial experience. Use your children as you would to go on the rides at an amusement park or to see the animated movie that requires a youngster in tow to avoid embarrassment. What may appear silly and foreign has far more meaning when you bother to learn about it. The child will not prejudge cultural events. After initial exposure they will be viewed as the norm, as what is expected.

But what of mixed marriages? What if one parent is Catholic and one Protestant? What if one is Italian and the other Irish? What if one is black and the other white? How can the children of such marriages develop a sense of extended belonging? If one parent does not care and the other does, the primary cultural attachment can be to the heritage of the parent who cares. If both parents are involved on this level, both connections should be made. Frequently one parent does have cultural group identity and the other is opposed to any such ethnic or religious involvements. The parent in opposition can be helped to see that the religious doctrines or cultural traditions are secondary to a sense of belonging for the child. Just bear in mind that a need to belong is close to universal. Without it, conditions for depression exist in the individual and the group. If the membership is to a group dedicated to love and caring, there is little to fear. If the membership is to a group dedicated to hatred and bigotry, the child will suffer. Delinquent gangs or ethnic, racial, and religious hate groups are another alternative. Why risk the latter?

Belonging is anti-cancer if the belonging goes beyond superficiality. If P.T.A. is the best you can do, you are not really belonging in the sense I speak of. Being a Republican or Democrat certainly has little value in this regard. Worse still is taking politics to the extreme. Being a congressman, senator, or even president seems to be so overwhelming that it is not uncommon for us to hear of divorce, adultery, alcoholism, and cancer as possible outcomes. These jobs and their group membership are anything but superficial. However, people who need such control, such power, and such responsibility are placing themselves in a role of absorbing devastating amounts of emotional irritation from their constituents. Such employment is certainly high risk.

When people do belong, primarily in a marriage and family and secondarily in a larger group, the cancer rates are lower. The larger group is the extended family in most areas of the world. Wherever the extended family exists the cancer rates are lower. Wherever the extended family exists there is a clanlike or tribal existence. This tribalism is also anti-cancer. People who lack a life of tribalism are far more likely to develop cancers. Nomads in Africa and Asia are always moving. But unlike Americans, they are never uprooted. The nomadic Arab or Mongol moves with the family, the extended family, and the tribe. American nomads

147

leave the family behind to move to a better job or a sunnier retirement village. If the American life-style has destroyed the extended family, we must reinstitute surrogate extended families. Neighborhood functions, service groups, caring for each other is all it takes.

But it is not enough just to heap similar people together. We still have ghetto environments. If these similar people do not experience a life-style of belonging to each other, it will make no difference that they live in close proximity. It is true that a black first meeting another black is probably far more comfortable than a black meeting a white the first time. This holds true for any group; Jews meeting Jews, Italians meeting Italians, Anglo-Saxons meeting Anglo-Saxons, or Asians meeting Asians. Once the individual is assessed, people who do not, as a rule, hate can view the different individual as just that, an individual. But without tribalism this reaction, comfort with same kind, is superficial at best. It appears to have no effect on people who lack the experience of real extended belonging. Teach your children to belong by setting the example.

Mormons are experts at belonging. They teach their children that the family takes precedence over all else. From birth onward they advocate moderation in all things. Alcohol, tobacco, and caffeine are prohibited. More important than these restrictions is the belonging that is inculcated from birth onward. When a Mormon family relocates, for whatever reason, they are immediately accepted into the fold in the new community. Friends and genuine caring are immediately accessible. And the Mormons, as a group, get cancer 23 percent less than the rest of America. And this reduced rate of cancer pertains to cancer not associated with alcohol, tobacco, or caffeine. They consume more red meat than many other Americans. They do not get cancer associated with such a diet at the same levels as many other people.

Among Mormons marriage is important, and extramarital or even premarital sex is shunned. Masturbation is viewed as an evil of self-containment. Divorce is frowned upon. Children are viewed as sacred treasures to be cared for with all of one's capacity for love. Their marriages seem to thrive on caring for children. They know how to have fun with their children and spouses. Plain and simple, they belong, family and marriage matters, and they genuinely care about one another. Add to this a life-style of actually belonging to the larger group and the anti-cancer life-style is spelled out. They have a 23 percent lower cancer rate regardless of where they live—even in the face of pollution or nuclear fallout, they experience far lower rates than their neighbors.

Most of us, however, are living in a time of social uncertainty. Confusion over what is important still pervades many households. Many problems have arisen out of this rapid rate of change. The family has become one major casualty. Feelings of sexual inadequacy are extensive. Psychoanalysts are like medics in this emotionally tumultuous time. We get to pick up the pieces.

But there are many benefits that have evolved from this cauldron of change. Parents now seem more interested in what science and research is discovering about pregnancy and child development. More and more is written—some of it naive garbage, but some of it urgently important. One of the most beneficial results of our changing roles is that men and women can be more comfortable in being involved with their children of the opposite sex. A father can play with dolls with his young daughters and a mother can coach her son's soccer team. Best of all, the girls can have their soccer team too, and a young boy will not immediately have a doll snatched out of his arms. Girls can be taught to be more comfortable with aggression, and boys can be taught to be more capable of showing love. In both cases the outcome will be a lowered risk of cancer. And the best part is how much fun the parents can have learning these previously sex-role-determined activities. Fathers can teach their wives and daughters or sons how to hit a softball. Mothers can teach their husbands and children how to bake from scratch. Many women already know how to play baseball, and may be better at it than Daddy. Many men have gotten into gourmet cooking and can teach their children and wives a thing or two.

By the time a child reaches two or three, he or she is capable of cause and effect thinking. At this point, teaching and learning can be so much fun because of the youngster's ability to reason. Loving parents delight in what the child can accomplish. And sharing and pride can exist in a marriage as both spouses watch this development.

Sharing of the child can be enhanced as one parent sees the other in the baby or toddler. Junior may have daddy's chin and mommy's eyes. The child represents the epitome of the infantile fusion and sharing that takes place in a happy marriage. The child is a constant reminder of the loyalty and connection within the marriage. Violations of loyalty to the marriage are now also violations to the bond with the child. One does not only cheat on a spouse. If the children can be shared and appreciated by both parents, I do not believe it is possible to have such violations. The two factors are really mutually exclusive.

THERE ARE TIMES in child rearing when the child very naturally attempts to destroy the marriage. Between the ages of three and seven children are more attached to the parent of the opposite sex in some regards. Jenny made this clear. At the age of five she told her mother that she, the mother, should go live with Grandma.

Mom: And who is going to take care of you?

Jenny: I will and if I want, Daddy will too.

Mom: But I'll miss you both a lot. I don't think I could stand that.

Jenny: Then will you move out of here? (Here being parents' bedroom.)

Mom: Where would I sleep?

Jenny: In my room.
Mom: Then where would you sleep?
Jenny: Right here, with Daddy.

Here mother could have laughed or attacked her. Instead she responded:

Mom: When you grow up and get married, you can marry and sleep with a man just like Daddy. He is wonderful, but he is my husband. Someday you can have a man just like him.

Twelve years later a similar situation exists. Jennifer (she does not like "Jenny" any longer) asks Mom for the car for Saturday night.

Jennifer: But Dad said I could have it. I told him I needed it three days ago. The girls are counting on me.
Mom: Let me just check with him then.
Jennifer: You know him, he doesn't remember anything. He'll tell you he never said it.
Mom: Well, I'll speak with your Dad anyway. He's not such an airhead. Who are you kidding?

Teenagers especially, but younger children as well, frequently use the battle cry of "But Dad said so." Before you fall for this entrapment simply talk to each other. Don't assume the child would not lie. It is to be expected.

At times lying is an expression of tact. Do you really want to hear about your daughter's sexual activities even with a young man she will probably marry? Do you *really* want to know why your son was out so late? The youthful need for adventure may frighten parents to no end, but there really is close to nothing you can do about it if you have not already taught basic good sense. Teenagers cannot be watched all the time. Drugs and alcohol and more liberal sexuality do exist. By the time a person reaches adolescence good sense about this had better have been taught. Adolescence is a dangerous time. Military experts prefer eighteen or nineteen year olds to twenty-five year olds for combat. The younger the soldier the more risks he will be willing to take. How anyone survives the normal risk-taking of adolescence is one of the amazing phenomena of life. Survival is based upon a sense of being loved from much earlier stages in life.

The teenager who is not involved with some excitement and some sense of belonging is a potentially dangerously depressed individual. Superficial friendships, a lack of interest in the opposite sex, lethargy, over- or undereating, self-indulgent drug or alcohol abuse, poor sleep habits, and general feelings of not enjoying things are all danger signals of serious depression. The adolescent who stays this way for even several weeks or months should be provided with professional help. Teenage suicide is tied in with the kind of pushing-away depression I have previously described. Depressed teenagers are also at significant risk for the development of cancer.

Part of the best way parents have of avoiding being set up, as well as helping the child avoid depression, is by setting limits. By the time the child is one and a half to two, limits can be set. The earliest limit setting is to protect the child. Before the child can anticipate the consequences of dangerous behavior, the parents must intervene. And before the parent loses control of his or her own impulses, limits must be set. By the time adolescence is reached, if limits have been set in order to love and protect the child, the child will have internalized these values. She will be able to set her own protective limits. She will be the one to pass up drugs or promiscuity. She will not drive drunk or with anyone else who is. She may pooh-pooh parental concern, but she will have a sense of self-preservation and ethics. Yes, there will still be rebellion. Rebellion at this stage is mostly wing stretching and testing. The testing is to find whether you still love the child.

Teenagers and young adults can paradoxically only mature and leave loving parents. If the parenting was negative or absent, the person can never really leave, never really let go.

Having worked in a state psychiatric hospital for several years, I can recall being startled by this phenomenon. There was fifty-year-old Alice wearing childlike clothes waiting for her sixty-eight-year-old mother to visit. When she did, Alice spoke in a toddlerlike voice, calling her Mommy. This was not unusual for these institutionalized psychotic people who had highly inadequate parenting early in life.

Children only leave good parents. If some day you wish to be rid of the responsibility for them, work at being a good parent. The rest of your life they can be there and be connected, but they will be able to care for themselves.

8

Carcinogenic Versus Anti-Cancer Marriage

"You don't know what you are talking about."
"Must you?"
"Oh, God, here we go again."
"Enough already."
"Get off my back."
"No way."
"Shut up."
"I don't want to hear it."
"That's ridiculous."
"You're crazy."
"We better stop talking about this."
"I need more time alone."

THESE ARE CARCINOGENIC communications designed to end any further communications. They are frequent phrases in marriages in which one, or both, partner is at risk. If either of you relates to the other in these ways, take it as a danger sign. Their outcome inevitably must be an internalization of feelings. Stewing in one's own juices, or eating one's self up alive will be characteristic for both spouses. It indicates a high level of internal irritants. The upset cannot be shared, and the marriage at this point is anything but fusional.

When the frequent phrases are designed to increase communication the marriage is most likely anti-cancerous.

> "Talk to me."
> "I need a hug."
> "What would make you feel better?"
> "When you do that, it's great."
> "I don't understand, explain."
> "Do you have any ideas?"
> "That was something, wasn't it?"
> "What do you think about this?"
> "What did you think of that movie [or book, or person, or anything]?"
> "Hold it a minute, nothing is worth this upset."

A marriage with open-ended communication such as these is based on a respect for each other's feelings. The partners are friends who enjoy talking. They can gossip with each other. They can share their fears and anxieties. They can stop conflicts when they start to get out of proportion to the issues. They can appreciate each other's opinions. When really important and emotionally laden problems arise, they are prepared. They have been talking and exchanging opinions as a normal part of their relationship. When problems at work or on the home front occur, talking is normal. They do not retreat into themselves. When tragedy or loss occurs, they are already prepared to communicate and soothe and comfort each other. They care about the other's thoughts and feelings. Their ideas and emotions blend together and each one's irritations are thus diluted.

A spouse who says, "I didn't like what happened between us, let's talk," is dedicated to making things work. Even if an answer is not immediately available, just wanting to make things better is enough to change feelings around. Words are important primarily because they provide the test to see if physical closeness is safe. Words are a testing of the waters. Physical closeness and gestures can many times be more effective than any words. When a spouse comes home terribly upset, the first communication may be in words. Something as benign as "How are you" may be met with an outburst or a shrug. Both indicate a need to push away. Stay with him or her. Perhaps a smile will start the letting go, then a hand can be placed on the shoulder, the neck rub may safely follow. Words can test the safety to approach, but the physical touch is what makes the real difference. If a picture is worth a thousand words, a hug is worth a million. What actually gets said is secondary to how things are said. The tone, the inflections, all contribute to the feelings. The content of the verbal communication is almost always close to irrelevant. The feelings are never irrelevant. You can tell your spouse that you hate him and hope he drops dead. If the tone is serious, look for an attorney. If the tone is joking or teasing, perhaps even sexy, the actual words won't matter.

In 1985, research by Richard Edelson and Joseph Fink demonstrated that T-lymphocytes reside and mature within the deeper structures of the skin. The skin is the ultimate barrier and protective organ. It works as the first line of defense in the body's immune system. Until recently it was viewed as just a passive barrier. Edelson and Fink have added significant information to our understanding of the interaction of the skin to the rest of the immune system. T-lymphocytes are white blood cells that function to destroy things like bacteria, cancer cells, and transplanted organs the body senses as not belonging. It was assumed that they grow only in the thymus gland and stay within the bloodstream. Now we have this potentially very important discovery to consider: T-lymphocytes are waiting in the skin like troops in reserve. Could this mean that touch could somehow liberate these cells to increase the efficiency of the immune system? Could

157

this help explain why having touch suddenly removed from one's life increases the risks of all sorts of disorders, cancer included? Could this explain the healing touch that many nursing students are now being taught? And could this also explain why sexual, touching, caring marriages can help keep people healthier in general? We cannot be certain, but all this does seem quite plausible. There is no way to overemphasize the importance of touching. As we get older it happens less and is needed more.

By the time a person reaches the age of forty, physiological changes occur that make people more vulnerable to their environment, both internally and externally. Far more exercise and far less food intake is required to make up for metabolic changes and maintain the body weight of a dozen years earlier. Unfortunately, as people do get older, exercise seems to decrease and food intake seems to increase.

Cellular changes also occur. Again, metabolism and the endocrine system in general affect the rate of normal cell division. When a youngster unfortunately fractures a bone, we frequently hear people refer to how fast the child mends. This translates to how rapidly cells are dividing under the influence of healing hormones. It is fast. After age forty it is much slower, and fractures are viewed as more serious.

The genetic material within the cells by age forty is becoming less stable. Fortunately, hormone levels are steadily decreasing. With unstable genetic material it's a good thing hormone levels are lower. There are thus fewer internal irritants to trip any precancerous land mines. Bodies now have less ability to heal and fight infections. Typically, they are simply not as fit. All of these factors contribute to increased health risks. After forty, the incidence of heart attack, cancer, and other degenerative disorders greatly increases. After forty, physicians may give electrocardiograms and cholesterol checks for the first time. Everyone knows this, especially insurance companies. With such greater risks, what is it that permits anyone to survive past forty? Biologically the decrease in hormones is vitally important. But every available statistic indicates *marriage* promotes longevity. Marriage directly influences the biology of the partners, hormone levels included.

ROZ IS FORTY-FOUR years old. She has two daughters in college. Next year her older girl graduates and her son starts. Next year she will be left with just her husband, Bert. Roz decided that she always wanted to live by a body of water. The house they now have is large and cumbersome. She thought they could move after their son left for college. One more year and the timing would be perfect. They could put away some more money to decrease the mortgage they would require.

Bert liked the idea, and if he could not live on a sprawling farm with a babbling brook and plenty of wooded acres in which to pursue his beloved grouse, then a waterfront would be just fine. Bert was sufficiently realistic to know that his nirvanna would require giving up his job, which he was not prepared to do. The water was a good second best.

There was no real rush to start looking for a new home, but Roz got caught up in a homesteading fever. She checked out waterfront homes on lakes, rivers, canals, bays, and the ocean. Thank goodness only one ocean was available. There were, however, innumerable canals and lakes to consider. In view of this multitude of potential choices, she decided she might as well get an idea of what was available. She wanted to take her time and make the right decision. She figured that moving would be a major pain, and she wanted this move to last the rest of her life. She wanted to make the right decision.

She checked out the lakes and decided that was not for her. The rivers and canals just didn't have it. And the bay was filled with boats driven by what appeared to be numerous inebriated Captain Ahabs. The ocean, with its crashing waves, moonlit nights, sandy beach, and tranquility was where the rest of her life should be spent.

Roz searched and searched. She is a woman of perseverance.

After the first days she was discouraged but determined that within the year she would find her dream house. It happened, 362 days ahead of schedule. That weekend, she and Bert, along with the real estate agent, approached her oceanfront dream. The house was lovely. Bert was not crazy about the tiles on the den floor but that was minor. He could replace them himself. The master bedroom had an ocean view, as did the den and the kitchen. Best of all the price was reasonable. He was thrilled to think they could own such a lovely home. He was proud to think they could really afford it. His years of hard work paid off.

Lawyers and real estate agents started haggling. It got tense for a while, but an agreement was finally reached. The contract was signed and the closing depended only upon mortgage approval. "Depended upon mortgage approval" was the key phrase. While on vacation Roz had paid the mortgage late. And, in the past, when unexpected expenses arose, Roz paid the mortgage last. After all, the late charge penalty was only twenty dollars. In a pinch it seemed to make sense to pay other expenses first. At some credit bureau a computer begged to differ. Vacations, added medical expenses, or a new car, did not register on the computer. All that the computer computed was a late payment. Computers do not care why. They do not even care if every payment for over twenty years was paid before a penalty was charged.

Mrs. Cahil from the bank called and asked for Roz. Roz identified herself, and Mrs. Cahil explained that "We have a little problem." She explained that due to a "history" of late payments the mortgage application was denied. Under the guise of helpfulness, she sadistically added that it would be very difficult to acquire mortgage approval with such a history.

The phone call ended the crashing waves. The moonlit nights became hidden behind clouds. And the sand was covered with eelgrass and seaweed. At the same time these images flashed in Roz's mind, her nervous system reacted as if she were under attack. Her pupils dilated, her heart rate and blood pressure increased, and her bronchi (air tubes in her lungs) relaxed. Thick viscid saliva was secreted into her mouth as her digestive system slowed down. Sugar stored in her liver entered her bloodstream. Her urinary bladder relaxed and her sphincter constricted. Under the influence of adrenaline or nor-adrenaline her physiology reacted as if she were in grave danger. These biological reactions continued until she received a dose of tranquilizing drugs: Bert came home.

She told him how insensitive Mrs. Cahil had crushed her dreams. She told him how sadistic she seemed to be. Bert half seriously said she was probably green with envy. He felt that their credit history was at least average, if not better. Then he said he would check with every bank and finance firm in the country if need be. He reassured her that he would get them the mortgage. No tangible or even reasonable facts were stated. Behind his words was the fact that he was there for her. Roz's eyes were still bloodshot and watery. She looked up at him like a trembling deer or rabbit who has just escaped from the hunt. The adrenaline-based reaction began to subside, not because of what he said, but rather how he said it.

The administration of the tranquilizing drug continued as Bert walked over and hugged her. She cried into the nape of his neck as he rubbed her back. Finally she pushed away and just looked up at his eyes. The look said, "I love you." Words were not necessary. They may even have interfered with the feelings. He leaned over and kissed her nose. She hugged him again.

Perhaps T-lymphocyte levels had been elevated in her bloodstream from his loving touching. Her pupils did contract as her heart rate and blood pressure lowered. The bronchi in her lungs narrowed, and she felt suddenly hungry from the increase in gastric secretions and activity. She also felt a need to urinate as her bladder contracted and the sphincter relaxed.

This ancient tranquilizer, the Bert factor, is a natural part of human physiology. Acetylcholine gets secreted, and the part of the nervous system set up to do things other than fight or flee gets activated. Internal irritation is decreased. The immune system's efficiency is most probably increased. And Roz is being protected from internal carcinogens.

In order for a marriage to be anti-cancerous, this type of exchange must occur for both partners. One must function as the soothing mother and absorb the other's irritation only part of the time. Roz must be able to do the same for Bert when he is hyperirritated. She too must be the caring mother. If this is not the case, the system will be carcinogenic and the more mature appearing partner who absorbs the irritations chronically will be at great risk. Anyone married to a frequently hyperirritated baby inside an adult body will be the likely candidate for malignancy. Having to worry about the spouse's reaction most of the time is a tremendous strain. Marriage to such an individual is like being in a state of constant red alert. Men or women married to drug or alcohol abusers, gamblers, or simply chronically tense individuals are very likely to absorb enough irritation to cause some kind of physical disorder. All too often the disorder is cancer.

By the way, Roz and Bert paid a little more for a mortgage and got the house.

IN ADDITION TO all of these easily viewed biological problems associated with turning forty, there are the psychological contributions to the aging milestone. At this age, perhaps even earlier, we are confronted with our own mortality. When we reach forty, statistics indicate that in America more than half our lives are over. We face death. And for most people, death represents a separation, a leaving of people or things we love. Every cancer patient I have treated discussed death in these terms. Fears of death or annihilation are more pronounced in people whose lives were not enjoyed to satisfactory levels. If from birth onward love was an integral part of life, death can be more easily accepted. Forty is most dangerous for those who did not start life off in a loving way.

This fear of separating, which death encompasses, brings us back to feelings of the infantile depression. The infant in us will continue to repeat what is familiar. If a pushing-away depression was part of early infancy, then it will be repeated at any time separation seems a threat: adolescence, pregnancy, sickness, injury, and getting older.

There are psychiatric diagnoses for depressions of people over forty that blame just hormonal inbalances. More likely these melancholic reactions are a reawakening of earlier melancholy. Depression, with its characteristic lethargy or hyperactivity, loss of appetite or compulsive overeating, and inability to sleep or need for excessive sleep are not uncommon at this point in life. Things are just not enjoyable any longer. Productivity diminishes. But the more typical and perhaps more dangerous outcome of this pushing-away depression is the need to destroy relationships. In marriage this can easily be done by having affairs. It defuses things, it lets you know the opposite sex is still interested and gives you back a feeling of elevated self-esteem. I heartily recommend an affair for anyone who reaches the age of forty. I would make only one small suggestion: make sure it is with *your* husband or wife.

The kids are older now, perhaps they have even left home and hearth. Making love as you would with a new lover can more easily take place. The bedroom is no longer the only available place. I enjoyed hearing of a couple who went to "make out" in the backseat of the family station wagon.

Add excitement to your relationship and not just sexually. Take up a hobby neither one of you has tried. Share time together. If you do, you must talk and enjoy each other. A young couple who scuba dive together told me not being able to talk requires a whole new dimension in communication. Yes, they made love under water. She said it was not very comfortable, but it was exciting.

Dress to please each other. Knock off the balast and love handles. If she wants you to wear your hair a certain way, and it will not rival a punk Rocker's hairstyle, why not? If he likes dangling earrings as opposed to studs, why not?

At forty, if it has not happened already, clothing should be chosen to please one's mate. Shop together, it really can be fun. Buy each other sneaky gifts. A sneaky gift is one you will enjoy your spouse using. A certain perfume or cologne, lingerie, or silk pajamas all qualify as sneaky gifts.

In my general practice I have witnessed a remarkable phenomenon. People who renew marriage vows at around this age come alive with love, romance, and sexuality. It is a real statement of love and commitment. Women feel such gestures as representative of safety in the relationship. They then can give more. Men feel safer too. It probably reaffirms their desire to control their impulses to stray. Whatever the reasons, publicly restating marriage vows at forty lets you know your spouse still wants and cares for you.

But what if at this stage of marriage the prerequisite loving feelings are insufficient for such a public reaffirmation? What if boredom predominates the relationship? What if the passion, the pizazz seems all but gone? I would strongly recommend a more secular form of exchanging vows than a church can provide—the intramarital affair.

SIX YEARS AGO a patient presented a brilliant idea of how to revitalize a sagging marriage. Paige is now fifty-one years old. She looks younger and makes the necessary efforts to stay trim and well toned. High cheekbones, fair skin, and light eyes are a big help. Friends tell her she looks like Tammy Wynette. Friends also tell her she sounds like Tammy Wynette. Paige is a displaced Georgia peach who married a Yankee when she was attending college. Robby was also attending Emory when they decided that the events of over a hundred years before should be laid to rest. He finished school and went on to comfortable success as a salesman for a large printing company. Paige left college after her sophomore year and decided she wanted to have a career as a wife and mother. By the time they were in their forties, the boys were off at school. Robby Junior was pursuing a Ph.D. in neurophysiology, and Len was in his sophomore year at a state school in New York. Tuition had made things tight. Business and marriage remained stable. The household was somewhat empty. Candidly, both Paige and Robby were bored.

In a delightful Southern accent, Paige presented her solution to this common marital dilemma:

"I knew we were in the doldrums in our marriage. He left for work and gave me a peck on the cheek. He came home from work and gave me a peck on the cheek. He would ask about what went on that day and get the same old answers.

"At night we watched TV or sometimes read. I love to read novels about the South. As soon as an author mentions Spanish moss, I'm back in Georgia. Sometimes I imagine what it was like prior to and during the Civil War. So romantic. The men were all gentlemen in my fantasies, and then I look over at my Brooklyn-born Rhett Butler and chuckle to myself. He's no Southern belle's fantasy, but I do love him.

"Anyway, our marriage was really becoming a big nothing. And then I got this ridiculous idea. I was always into romantic fantasies but I'm not the type to act on them. Robby is like me, we're dull people. Well, at least we're average people. But no one ever fantasizes about average. You know how all those movie stars keep talking about their previous lives? How come none of them picture being just an average person in a previous existence? Even as movie stars, I guess they still feel insecure, so they have to come up with such a pack of horsefeathers.

"My fantasy started when I looked at an old family photo album. Robby was a strong, handsome-looking buck in those days. I wasn't bad myself. Anyway, I got the idea that we could do it all over again. I mean that we could date each other like we did as kids. I figured we could set up some rules to follow, and maybe it would work. I got so excited by this idea. I mean, you know, I'm not a wild person. The big thing in my life was being a baton twirler in high school. Like I said, I'm an average American woman. I was so nervous about telling Robby that it took over a week to get up my courage. I figured he'd laugh at me, but I was wrong. He got just as excited.

"That night we sat down and drew up the rules. Number one was that he had to take me out on dates. Number two was we had to act like we just met as best we could. We figured that to do this we were not allowed to talk of home, kids, or work. Number three was that while we "dated" we would have no sex at home. If anything happened we had to do it like kids, sneaking around. And the last rule was that we couldn't talk about the dating at home.

"The next afternoon I got a bouquet of flowers with a note from a secret admirer. The writing was not Robby's. Two days passed and nothing happened. It was Wednesday when he called before he came home from work. He said he felt stupid doing all this. I asked him if he ever wanted to have sex again. He asked me out to dinner and a concert. That weekend the most exciting thing in my life started to take place. I was to fall in love with my husband all over again.

"We got dressed in separate rooms. I left him our bedroom and used Robby Junior's old room. I bathed slowly and then got dressed. I put on new, red, lacey undies and then a clingy dress I bought without him knowing. I looked great. We arranged that he would pick me up and actually ring the front door bell. When I opened the door was I shocked. Robby had gotten contacts to replace his wire-rimmed coke-bottle glasses. He has very nice gray eyes when the coke bottles were off. The new contacts were tinted a deep blue. When I opened the door, I saw his eyes and couldn't stop staring. He was gorgeous. I started to say something, and he stopped me so I wouldn't ruin our game. He helped me on with my coat, held the door for me, and opened my side of the car first. When I was seated, he got in. He told me that I looked lovely. The game continued when he said blind dates in the past were always a disappointment, but that I was anything but.

"At the restaurant we had wine with our meal, and he held my hand. I asked him what he did for a living, and for the first time I actually found out. I mean I knew he was a salesman. But I never really knew what a printing salesman did or how this business worked. Magazine accounts were fascinating. I couldn't believe it, but I was really interested. When he asked me what I did, I told him I studied literature and was planning on writing my first novel. We discussed the plot, and it was fascinating. We were writing a story about what we were doing.

"The concert was delightful, but the walk on the winter beach was even nicer. When we got back to the car we were cold, and while the heater warmed up he started to rub my shoulders real fast. The rubbing got slower and slower. He kissed me so gently, as if he were afraid. I kissed back more powerfully. There I was with my husband of twenty-five years making out in a parking lot at Jones' Beach. He unbuttoned my coat and reached for his second favorite part of my anatomy. I let him put his hand on the outside of my bra. I made sure he saw the red lace. When he tried to undo it, I stopped him. And when he went for his favorite part of my anatomy, I told him I really felt we shouldn't, that it was too soon. I thought he would be teed off, but he wasn't. We kissed good night at the front door. Half jokingly he asked if he could call me again. In the heaviest Southern drawl I could muster I said, 'Why Robby, I'd be honored.' We both laughed. That night we slept in the same bed without touching or talking about our date. I felt sorry for him. He was obviously more aroused than I had seen him in years.

"Other dates immediately followed. I felt so wanted. I couldn't wait to see those blue eyes in candlelight, or on a horse—yes, we even went horseback riding. We went into New York City and saw things we had never seen before. We went to the ballet, the theater, and the Empire State Building, but the best was riding the Staten Island Ferry back and forth all night. We ate in decent restaurants, but we didn't spend the money to go to the best. Chinatown was even more fun anyway.

"By our fourth date the making out had really progressed. We were actually concerned about getting caught by a cop in our car. I mean what could we say? The guy would have assumed we were married but probably not to each other.

"We started to work at looking good for each other. We both lost weight. We paid attention to how we dressed. I was working at seducing him, but I was also going slowly. Finally he gambled on a hotel room. I had some white wine and was feeling good. We played footsie in a piano bar at a ritzy hotel in Manhattan. He leaned over with those pleading blue eyes and told me he rented a room for the night. I demurely looked down and said okay. Well, I won't give you the blow by blow, but all I can say is it was worth waiting for. Isn't that ridiculous? But it is true. We were in a fever when we got there. Even so, we didn't do everything. I mean what kind of a girl do you think I am?

"By our sixth date, however, we did. It was wonderful. The best part is we got to really know each other. As first-time lovers we were able to slowly make it clear what we wanted. I found out things I never knew about him. He was a darling boy and only wanted to make me happy. And boy did he make me happy.

"It is six or seven years later now, but he still asks me out on dates. And I still dress to please him and can't wait to get him alone at these times. After the first two years of this I came to realize that I was having an affair with my husband. We couldn't be any happier or more in love."

AFTER THE AGE of forty, "newness" is important to help any marriage retain its excitement. But ten, twenty, or more years of living with another person certainly has its own benefits. By now a couple has learned to tolerate each other's imperfections. If the marriage is to be healthy, tolerance is required. If imperfections are a constant irritation, perhaps the irritated partner has a need to be in such a state. On occasion, one partner may be late, sick, or inconsiderate. If isolated incidents are harped upon, the need for irritation is most probably there!

When people marry and expect to change a spouse radically, one or the other is being set up for unhappiness. The choice of such a mate is designed to keep the adrenaline flowing. Yes, people will adapt, but basic traits are very unlikely to change. A marriage that has survived twenty years usually indicates that there is a concern for the partner's well-being. But on occasion people will marry and stay married to mates who clearly are not concerned. This repeats an early aberration of mother-infant bonding. Early exposure to neglect can set us up to unconsciously seek it later in life. Human beings are prisoners of what is familiar, not what is best.

We can and usually will repeat what was programmed into our nervous system from the most impressionable stage of life—early infancy. But things can change, and marriage, mature marriage, is one of the best ways to be reprogrammed internally.

The maternal, caring role must be alternated. If one partner is almost always in the infantile role and the other is always absorbing, the absorber of the emotional irritation will more likely develop cancer. Mutuality must exist. If this switching of roles does not take place, the original programming is going to be maintained. If roles are alternated, then a reprogramming can occur.

At forty it is a time to stop and examine such matters. Life will not go on forever, and if you are dissatisfied now is the time to work for change. Now is the time to behave differently so that feelings in both of you can change. If by now the oppositeness of your spouse's gender is not important to you, work to make it so. Men and women are not the same. Whether society or biology establishes these differences does not matter in making a marriage better.

In recent research by Amy Munroe and Dr. Neil Jacobson of the

University of Washington, this was made crystal clear. Women were consistently shown to be far more interested in the motivation, the "whys" of their husband's behaviors. Women are more interested in understanding the good qualities as well as the negative aspects of their men. They spend time thinking about such things. Men, on the other hand, even happily married men, do not devote much mental energy to such concerns unless they are really jolted out of their complacency by some sort of conflict.

Once the marriage starts to turn sour, both husbands and wives look for causes. If your marriage is basically good, your mate's irritation will be viewed as coming from a temporary situation. If, for example, he comes home crabby and hostile, a wife who is mostly contented will see this as a result of a tough day at work. If the marriage is distressed, the wife may see this crabbiness as further proof of what a pain in the neck she married.

When good things happen in a contented marriage, Munroe and Jacobson point out that the spouse will see it as coming from the positive attributes of the other partner. If the marriage is unhappy, occasional good things will be seen as due to the situation or for ulterior motives. Problems get perpetuated by such perspectives. In order to change things one or both partners must alter behavior for a prolonged period of time.

When people tell me they are willing to give an idea a shot, I know they will most likely fail. Change requires consistent repetition. The other thing I hate to hear is that one or both partners are "willing to try." This implies an unconscious need to fail. If you decide to use a new tactic, do it, don't try it.

It is true that women seem more oriented toward seeking an understanding. Men are frequently oriented toward taking action. I am not suggesting this is a good state of affairs. It is just the way it is.

By the age of forty or fifty certainly some of the insecurities of youth can be laid aside. In so doing, women can be more active and men can be more understanding. It is a time in life that is optimum for change. The dissatisfactions of the past can be replaced through better, less threatened communication, and through more definitive actions. Empathy, respect, and a sharing can be far more pronounced in the older couple. But they cannot replace excitement and passion. With passion, love, and involvement, then sharing, empathy, and caring cannot help but happen. If these qualities have not been there, take a chance and follow Paige's example. The worst that can happen is a continuation of what has already happened. The good is not likely to get bad, and the bad quite possibly will get good. Take a chance!

But what of the apparently ideal marriage of two very nice people that ends in the midlife crisis of adultery and frequently divorce. These are the kinds of situations that shock everyone who knows the couple. They may be comfortable with affection. Their sexual existence may be more than satisfactory. They may appear to be very much in love. Oddly enough they may actually feel very much in love. So then why should any marriage like this end in adultery and divorce?

The answer again lies in the very early learning to which an infant's nervous system can be subjected. If the baby came to expect irritation when already hyperirritated, the adult will expect the same. If the baby learned to avoid connecting to an irritating maternal figure, the adult will be able to connect but will consistently feel irritated when doing so. The marriage may have all the right ingredients except one—one or both partners who are comfortable with closeness. The need to be antifusional will have to be played out. Reality and good common sense will have nothing to do with it.

GARY IS SUCH a man. He is not comfortable with closeness. He was a very good baby, a very good boy, and appears to be a very good man. He learned very early in life not to provoke. He learned to be as perfect as possible, and he learned to be in control. He is a

171

powerful but gentle personality. The power seems to get people to do what he wants. It gets people to agree with him. And most important, it keeps him protected from assumed dangers in his social environment. Having always been this way, he is totally unaware of any of this. He has no idea of the effect he has on others. He sees himself as a kind, giving person. Others, his wife, Phyllis, included, see him the same way.

As they approach fifty, their marriage is close to perfect. They genuinely care for each other. Neither one is the least bit inhibited, and their frequent sexual contacts are thoroughly enjoyable. Gary has never forgotten a birthday or anniversary. The two of them have been contenders in several mixed doubles tournaments. They hold hands and hug in public, at parties, or just walking down the street.

Since their sixteenth anniversary, Gary has had nineteen extramarital sexual relationships. None of these women was particularly more attractive, sexually adept, or more loving than Phyllis. If you ask him why these indiscretions, he says he must just need variety. If you push the issue, he says he honestly does not know. At this point he admits to feeling guilty and even "crazy." Gary can see what an excellent relationship he has with Phyllis. What he cannot see is that Phyllis represents an early maternal figure as well as a wife and lover. Unconsciously he finds Phyllis dangerous. Any woman would be dangerous once Gary began to connect emotionally. As this level of relating is approached, the pushing-away or infantile depression gets activated. His nervous system is defending against anticipated impingement from his now surrogate mother.

If you point out the reality of Phyllis's love for him, if you point out how she has never really hurt him, he can only respond by saying, "I know, I know." He is confused and overwrought by the situation. To relieve some of his upset over his actions he asks, "Don't you think I feel crazy over this? Phyllis is an angel. Sex is great with her, and none of these others are as good. I know I should stop doing this, but I just can't. If a beautiful young piece of ass is available, I know I'll jump on her. I know I don't really want to. So what the hell is going on with me. It's like I'm a junky."

Gary is really in pain. When he compares himself to a junky, he does not realize how accurate he may be. Whenever a person becomes depressed, the use of drugs, alcohol, gambling, or promiscuity may be to cover up or escape from this high level of internal irritation. Take away addictive behavior and you are always left with a very irritated, very depressed human being. In treatment it is necessary to do just that so that the irritation and depression can be dealt with. Timing is, however, all important. If you take away the cover-up too soon, the person may become completely overwhelmed. Alcoholics and drug addicts being detoxified are genuinely going through hell, the hell of hyperirritation and infantile depression. Promiscuous people who give up such behavior must confront their feelings. The same holds true for compulsive gamblers. Drugs, alcohol, gambling, and promiscuity can all be used to make relationships anti-fusional. They can easily destroy anyone's ability to relate to a loved one.

The abuser is extremely self-centered when involved with such defenses. He will frequently argue that his behavior is not going to hurt anyone. If the parents or, later in life, the spouse do not consciously know about his behavior the acting-out person can rationalize that he is not hurting anyone.

In my opinion, such covers for depression are always harmful to others. Husbands and wives may not know but can almost always sense when their spouses are disloyal. Women seem to be more capable of this sensing. And this sensing has biochemical consequences. The systems stay chronically poised to confront a threat. Sexual organ systems become the frequent site of cancer. Other organ systems are also vulnerable to this steady onslaught of internal carcinogens. Don't fool yourself into believing that a spouse of twenty years can really be deceived. She may deceive herself consciously, but her involuntary nervous system cannot be deceived or denied even by herself.

The infantile depression may be very painfully activated when the acting-out partner stops the acting out. But if the marriage is a really good one, your spouse will see you through. In reality, allowing access to this depression is the only way to stand a chance of correcting it. And a loving husband or wife may finally be able to provide the right feelings that were not present in infancy. Besides, by allowing this emotional reeducation, the innocent spouse is being protected.

BESIDES ADOLESCENCE AND reaching the age of forty, another event in life can abruptly bring an individual face to face with infantile depression. When cancer is diagnosed, infantile depression coupled with hyperirritability becomes a universal psychological response. If these psychological phenomena can be effectively dealt with, I believe almost any cancer can be reversed. Resolving this pushing-away depression appears to change the patient's biochemistry and to maximize the immune system. For the last ten years of treating cancer patients, my colleagues and I have observed elevated white cell counts in every patient whose depression gets resolved, even partially resolved. Probably the endocrine functions also change beneficially. As yet, we have not documented these endocrine shifts. Such tests are not normally done for cancer patients, but complete white cell counts are routinely performed.

Relationships, marital relationships particularly, seem to provide powerful contributions to reversing "hopeless" cancer. In almost every case of people defeating cancer that they were told could not be defeated, their spouses played a critical role. The diagnosis of cancer can so thoroughly shake people up that they go through radical emotional changes. If they do the chances of beating cancer greatly increase. But if the cancer makes already established behavior patterns even more powerfully ingrained, the cancer will win every time.

Bear in mind that guilt has no value in dealing with cancer in a marriage. If however, extramarital sex, alcohol, gambling, obesity, or rejection have been a significant aspect of a marriage in which one spouse develops cancer, the perpetrator should feel guilty. If you are having an extramarital affair and your wife develops breast or cervical cancer, you should feel very guilty. If you chronically reject your husband's sexual advances and he develops prostate cancer, guilt is a very appropriate feeling.

It is true that the precancerous land mines get set up in infancy. And it is true that people do not intentionally cause cancer in their spouses. But now that you understand how cancer can be triggered, you must take responsibility for having or not having a carcinogenic marriage.

Having an anti-cancer marriage is within reach. Not only is it a definite possibility, it also makes for a much happier life in general.

9

Aging: A Continuation of the Anti-Cancer Marriage

> ... Doctor Thomas sat over his dinner
>   Though his wife was waiting to ring,
> Rolling his bread into pellets,
>   Said, "Cancer's a funny thing.
>
> Nobody knows what the cause is,
>   Though some pretend they do!
> It's like some hidden assassin
>   Waiting to strike at you.
>
> Childless women get it,
>   And men when they retire.
> It's as if there had to be some outlet
>   For their foiled creative fire ..."
>
> —W. H. Auden in "Miss Gee"

WHEN AUDEN WROTE THIS provocative poem, the work of geneticists and microbiologists such as Robert Weinberg, Michael Wigler, and Barbara McClintock was not yet known.

They have shed some very bright light onto our understanding of what the causes are. We now know that the instability of genetic material is almost a certainty in the evolution of cancer. We now know that genetic material is not rigidly stable.

Cancer is a disorder of the genetic material. In Western societies cancer occurs most frequently in the young and the elderly. In youth this instability is most likely due to the rapid rate of cell reproduction that characterizes growth. In the elderly, this instability appears to be connected to degeneration of this genetic material and/or the accumulation of carcinogens over the years.

The fact is that of all the people who die from cancer worldwide, only 2 percent are younger than thirty. Thus, cancer has been largely classified as a disorder of the elderly. But survival and growing old seem carcinogenic only in industrialized societies. In the Crimea, Peru, the Caucasus Mountains, and the rural valleys of Italy, growing old and avoiding cancer does not seem to be much of a challenge.

After all, in the Andes or the Caucasus Mountains people are not concerned about high yield money market funds or rushing to the 5:40 train, and they get married and stay married. At the age when a person is ready for retirement in America, people are just reaching their prime in these other societies. A death for any reason below the age of ninety or one hundred may very well be considered a tragic early loss.

In our nation, which is thirty-third for male longevity in the world, making it to seventy-three is considered quite satisfactory. In these other societies where there is a definite place for the elderly, seventy-three is still young.

The extended family assures a place of respect and love for the great-great grandparents. They belong and are wanted. They also do not abandon their offspring for retirement communities in the sunbelt.

The elderly are viewed as valuable members of the community, as the teachers of the traditions that help bind a people together, as wise ones to help solve problems, as the technical instructors in the fine arts of survival, and as the treasure trove of information that they are.

In a high tech society, change is so rapid it is hard to connect yesterday with today. By the time tomorrow evolves, yesterday is the old way. Old implies bad. New and innovative become the watchwords. We continue to "progress" and we continue to lose our foundations. We border on being a society totally devoid of all the benefits of past learning.

But what if the United States and other Western nations had very specific reasons for not wanting its citizens to live any longer than they already do?

By the 1960s, no questions remained in connecting cigarette smoking with lung cancer, cardiovascular disorders, or emphysema. Oddly enough, in the years that followed very little has been done to curb the tobacco industry. More young women are smoking now than ever before, and each of the packs of cigarettes they purchase is taxed. Federal and state cigarette taxes amount to well over $5 billion a year. Most important for the high tech thinkers in America's and Great Britain's governments, cigarettes result in fiscal solvency. The cost of benefits for the elderly is greatly reduced if the elderly do not get much more elderly, and huge savings are achieved. That's correct—old age benefits would financially cripple America and Britain if people lived much longer. And cigarettes, with significant exceptions, reduce longevity. The U.S. government is saved approximately $35 thousand in Social Security payments for each smoker in America. Most of the deaths are not from lung cancer, but instead from cardiovascular and other chronic lung disorders. This reduction in life span translates to approximately $10 billion a year in old age benefits.

Yes, we all know of people who reach very old age and have always smoked and drank. But the statistical analysis clearly indicates that both cut down on life expectancy. The people in nations like America and Britain who seem to get away with it more often than not are the Walters and Hannahs who remain connected to their very positive early infancies throughout their marital and family lives. This life-style appears to combat the cumulative effects of carcinogens.

The battering that large amounts of cigarette smoke, sunlight, bacon, or pollution over the years can do to the body can be cumulative. If at the same time the person is involved in a carcinogenic marriage, or no marriage at all, the level of internal irritants will be chronically high. Add the two together and the likelihood of a cancerous explosion is greatly increased. Subtract the internal carcinogen level from this deadly total, and only the external remains. We can now see why some people can work in an asbestos factory for twenty years and not get cancer. And we can see why others can work there for only twenty weeks and get cancer. How the irritation gets processed is certainly more important than what the irritation is.

In my opinion, and the opinion of many research biologists, for cancer to develop the cell must go through certain stages when exposed to irritants. First the cell must get set-up for later shifting of genetic material. I believe that this setup occurs at the most vulnerable time in life—early infancy. Taking this into account, we can tie the psychology to the biology of people who get cancers. Both are set-up in infancy. The psychology will continue to have a pattern of seeking irritation both internally and externally. Taking a job that is very irritating physically or emotionally is a setup. No one is really the prisoner of an assembly line, law firm, or medical practice. Plenty of people change occupations in midlife or even later.

The "foiled creative fire" that our poet Auden referred to is more precisely the lack of fulfillment that the infantile depressed person experiences for a lifetime. Many childless women and retired men suffer from enormous feelings of not having or losing something very dear. If emotions are strongly attached to whatever is experienced as lost, the risk of cancer increases. The cancers of Robert Taft, Hubert Humphrey, Ulysses S. Grant, and Napoleon can easily be tied to the emotional loss of political defeat. The greatest carcinogen for the elderly is loss. We will discuss how to best cope with the loss of a loved one or job later. Right now, because the elderly in Western societies are at greatest risk of developing cancer we must discuss some vital facts of cancer that will help in treating and coping with this disorder.

First and foremost, cancer prevention, particularly for the elderly, is where our emphasis should be. Within the United States, groups such as the Mormons and Seventh-Day Aventists suffer from far fewer cancers. Prevention based upon life-style is within everyone's reach.

Almost no leading death-causing disorders have been effectively dealt with by treatment. That is right: almost no serious disorders have been reduced or eliminated through treatment. When they have been effectively dealt with, prevention is almost always the way. Cholera, pellagra, typhus, malaria, scurvy, and, as I mentioned previously, tuberculosis have faded in America because we have learned how to prevent them, not because they can be treated. Cardiovascular diseases have recently begun to decline in the United States due to life-style changes that aid in prevention. Polio has been reduced through vaccination rather than treatment. There is no historical precedent on which to base emphasizing treatment over prevention. Yet the major investment of government and established cancer organizations is still in the area of treatment. Clearly the priority should be for prevention. The problem is that like increased longevity, prevention costs too much on the governmental level.

It is true that screening programs and early detection are of value only for those cancers that have a clear and prolonged precancerous state (the use of Pap smears for abnormal cell growth in the cervix) or for those cancers that stay localized for a sufficient length of time to be detected before they have spread (many breast and prostate cancers).

However, for some cancers, early detection *seems* to make

181

sense, for others, it is an unwarranted additional danger. Treatment is the watchword of the medical professions. The physician who can tell a patient that he has no means of helping (when that is the case) is worth his weight in gold. When all the studies indicate that the treatments available provide no beneficial gains, it is the ethical and moral obligation for physicians to stop grasping at straws. The patient's comfort should take precedence.

But when a doctor must inform a patient that he has no effective treatment for this cancer, hope should not be taken away. The truth is that people do beat "hopeless" cancer, not often enough but enough to raise serious questions as to why.

From my experience the people who have experienced spontaneous cures have four things in common. Number one, they forced themselves to eat. Number two, they moved; staying in bed was seen as lethal. Number three, they related to others even if it meant cutting back on pain medication to do so. Number four is the least obvious and perhaps the most important. They had spouses who interfered with their previous patterns of managing irritation. Someone was there for them.

EVERYONE SHOULD KNOW the facts behind the recommended medical treatments for cancer. In addition to surgery, cancer is treated through radiotherapy and chemotherapy. Let's start with radiotherapy.

In 1895, Wilhelm Roentgen discovered X rays, and almost immediately X rays were seen to cause damage to human tissues. In localized cancer, x-radiation makes sense. We now know the tolerance levels for each area of the body, so we can now concentrate the X rays with far greater precision than previously. Cancers that are very sensitive to radiation can be successfully treated. These include Hodgkin's disease, a specific type of testicular cancer, and cancer of the cervix. In order for successful treatment to occur, the cancer must be significantly more sensitive to radiation than the normal cells that surround it. If too

182

much of the body must be exposed, then the immune system gets attacked as does the bone marrow. Risk versus benefit, as in all medical cancer treatment, must be carefully weighed.

Chemotherapy is the next major approach in the field of oncology (cancer treatment). These chemicals are referred to as cytotoxins, which simply means they poison cells. The idea is to poison cells that reproduce rapidly. Cancer cells reproduce rapidly but so do the digestive tract lining and hair follicles. All of the chemicals used attack the genetic structures to cause cell death.

Early work in the field of childhood leukemia and lymphoma helped establish a very questionable precedent. It was found that the tiniest cancer that can be diagnosed has at least a billion cells present. This means that out of this minimum of a billion cells some will be different enough to resist the effect of any single poison. As a result, S.O.P. for today's chemotherapy is to use as much poison as can be tolerated and to use several different kinds at the same time.

With the proper combinations of poisons, many childhood cancers can now be cured. In 1950, about two thousand children died in the U.S.A. from cancer. The rate is down to seven hundred per year now. This is a significant degree of success. In older children and young adults, the cures have not been as significant. With the exception of certain testicular cancers, childhood leukemia, and Hodgkin's disease, death rates have not been affected over the years by chemotherapy. For the old and middle-aged, chemotherapy has been a disappointment.

Hormone-blocking treatments are another type of chemotherapy. In organs such as breasts and prostate glands, cancers can be affected by hormone-blocking agents. Tamoxifen is an estrogen-blocking agent that interferes with cancer cells' ability to use estrogen to foster rapid cell reproduction. Prostate cancer can be slowed by using estrogen. The nice part of hormonal treatments is that they have almost none of the negative side effects of other chemotherapies. For older women with breast cancer, most studies now indicate that the use of Tamoxifen alone is just as effective as when chemotherapy is used in conjunction with it.

IF YOU ARE an American, you have a one in three chance of personally facing cancer. If you are an older American, your risks are the greatest. You must read and educate yourself before there is a tangible need. Your objectivity cannot be relied upon if you or your spouse develops cancer.

For example, did you know that studies indicate that there is no increase in survival rates for people who receive chemotherapy versus those who do not, after being surgically treated for metastatic colorectal tumors? Chemotherapy at the least made the experimental groups very uncomfortable but did not increase longevity at all compared to the control group that did not receive it. If breast cancer is localized, many studies and doctors agree that chemotherapy is uncalled for since it significantly increases the chance of developing leukemia.

If medical treatment and even prevention have proven to be disappointments, innovative therapy that treats the mind and body is showing promise. In view of the fact that this adjunctive type of treatment cannot hurt, there is no reason not to include it along with other medical approaches. For hundreds of years, physicians have connected the mind and body to help fight all sorts of disorders. With cancer, this connection is not being adequately considered by modern society. High-tech thinking has disconnected the mind-body alliance.

To fight existing cancer successfully we must appreciate how the mind affects the internal chemical environment and the immune system. Until we regain respect for the endocrine and neuroimmune systems, cancer will continue to be, by and large, unsuccessfully prevented and treated.

The best way to deal with cancer within your marriage, however, is not to get it. If you have had a fusional marriage, there is a far better chance that cancer will never be a personal issue for either of you. To continue living within an anti-cancer marriage while growing older requires our additional consideration.

PARADOXICALLY, WHEN PEOPLE reach old age they tend to be less physically affectionate, and yet at this time of life their physiology requires more physical affection. Affection is the best way to keep adrenaline-based reactions and hormonal influences to a minimum. Affection and bonding are the best ways to keep the immune system as strong and efficient as possible.

In my interviews with older couples, I must admit surprise at how frequently people near or even over eighty said they were still "making love." One older gentleman explained how sex into old age was accomplished. Otto was born in the emperor's Austria seventy-one years ago. His family emigrated to Germany after World War I. As he put it, "Mein Vater was a fery great man. He just was not gut vit choices. So . . . ve vind up im Germany vhere tings are goink von vat to vorse.

"After gymnasium, high school im Amerika, I go to study massage im Baden-Baden. I get real gut. I make money von rich peoples. Den mein Vater to Amerika takes us. Ve are Lutheran but Vater was right dis time. In Amerika I meet mein schoner Ursala. She is beauty. Ve marry. Years later ve are at var mit Germany. Tanks Gott I do not haf to Germans fight. I teach instead officirien German to speak. Die Var ist ended und I vork in hospital mit GI's. I am P.T., physikal terapist. I start to massage rich peoples again. I make money. Ursala und me, we haf three kinder. Ve love to make shoner kinder. Ve love to make love. Ve alvays massage each odder. I teach her. Ve still love to touch and massage each odder. Ursala and I ve are fery happy people. Venn young ve like to make love; venn old ve love to do it. I hope venn I die it happens right after ve make love."

Otto is most likely not going to depart from this world in his chosen way. The truth is almost all men who die making love or immediately after are making love to someone other than their wives.

People like Otto and Ursala and Hannah and Walter surprise all of us. In retirement communities sex is a frequent topic of joking. Older people seem very comfortable with it. They seem to know intuitively that it somehow relates to longevity. If it is loving sex it is apparently very safe sex. Not having to worry about unwanted pregnancy adds to feelings of enjoyment.

Loving sex is perhaps our most powerful way of reinforcing a sense of belonging. After forty, fifty, or more years of marriage, still being wanted, desired, appreciated for one's physical being is life preserving. The sex again recapitulates early feelings of bonding. And just as important this sense of being wanted adds to the feelings we all should have had in our infancies. At any stage in life, feeling wanted is urgently important. When old age is reached, feeling wanted is perhaps even more important. The elderly are aware that they no longer look like "playmates of the month" or football heroes. They have been told by big corporations that they are no longer wanted. Even our social security system, which was established to help the elderly, prefers that they no longer make withdrawals from this dwindling fund. Departing this world on schedule is the only fiscally responsible way to manage this problem.

The absurd part of our culture's rejection of the elderly is what we lose by assuming this position. Since I began interviewing older couples for this book, I have spent hour upon hour being fascinated by what they could teach me. The elderly can teach all of us. All we as a nation must do is stop and listen. The obscenity of forced retirement has always deprived us of our best teachers. If the young and middle-aged can give older people a feeling of being appreciated and wanted, they will promote longevity. If the young and middle-aged can teach their own children to value them appropriately, they will promote their own longevity. In societies where elders are valued, people live longer. These societies seem to genuinely desire the knowledge age provides. The elderly are not just good as members of a society. They are vital to the survival of any society.

Now we are also experiencing rejection of the young by the elderly. Older people who are financially capable are retiring to sunbelt regions, deserting children and grandchildren. On occasion their children relocate with them to maintain the family and establish new lives in these lovely areas of America. We must, however, consider that change of almost any major kind, particularly for the elderly, can be correlated with cancer. Most important change that includes loss definitely and powerfully correlates with cancer. Relocation all too often means loss. Even more potentially dangerous than relocating is the phenomenon that frequently accompanies it—retirement.

Throughout life we think of ourselves as carpenters, doctors, farmers, librarians, teachers, lawyers, electricians, etc. Suddenly retirement means we are former somethings. The esteem we got from our labor is no longer there. Depression over this loss of esteem is not unusual. Depression that is prolonged and powerful is carcinogenic.

Equally important is the *loss* of the stress associated with many jobs. We all have heard of top-level executives who have functioned for years deeply immersed in stress. When they retire we have unfortunately heard of the rapid evolution of cancer. Stress for these people is anti-cancer. It prevents them from being in touch with inner conflicts that relate to anxiety from early infancy. Without the stress, these very irritating infantile feelings come forth. They are destructive through their stimulation of the production of internal carcinogens. Anxiety is more destructive than stress. Stress is from the outside; anxiety is from the inside.

If retirement is unavoidable, be oppositional—that is, switch from one area of emotional investment to another. This may mean leaving the boardroom for the volunteer position at the local hospital. It may mean leaving the household chores for assisting at a day care center. It may mean teaching younger professionals what the years have taught you. Or perhaps coaching new business people based on your experience. If you have used stress to contain anxiety, you cannot risk spending the rest of your life playing golf or bridge or going fishing. This will inevitably mean that the anxiety that the stress was hiding will come out. This can result in very powerful, painful feelings of hopelessness and despair.

However, if stress has not been part of your previous employment and life-style, retiring to recreation will probably be safe.

Another area to reinvest your emotions is in each other. This, however, is a somewhat ridiculous premise. If you have made it to being elderly as a couple, and if you are both healthy with no history of cancer or cardiovascular disorders, I certainly have nothing to add to your relationship. You obviously already know what works. Take pride in this. But be sure to continue what has worked for both of you. Be there as you always have been to comfort each other, particularly when dealing with loss. At these times the nonverbal ways of communicating will be even more important than words. But you already know all of this.

If one of you has suffered from a physical malady of any consequence, beware of the "yes, dear" syndrome. This occurs when a spouse is physically uncomfortable and becomes a cranky baby almost all the time. The spouse who evolves into a "yes, dearer" is now at greater risk of a malignancy. This spouse is serving as a repository for the emotional upsets of both spouses. It may be necessary to be very assertive, even if you have never been so before. A swift kick in the emotional butt can frequently work wonders on elderly cranky babies. This holds true for almost any stage of marriage but seems to work best for elderly couples.

Another bit of advice applies to young, middle-aged, and older couples. Total honesty has no place in marriage. Basic honesty, yes. Total honesty, no. When she asks about the new dress or hairdo that she obviously likes, if it is not ludicrous, tell her you

188

like it even if you don't. When he wants to know whether his new tennis or golf outfit looks good, lie, unless you will be embarrassed by his appearing in public looking like a Picasso cubist painting. This is called tact. It is necessary to make any marriage work. It is even more necessary for the elderly as insecurity about sexual functioning and physical appearance increases. Older people and very young people are very sensitive people.

MILDRED IS SEVENTY-SEVEN. She describes her husband's golf attire almost as well as George Burns could have.

"Ralph is a sweet guy. But he has been married to golf for longer than he is married to me. I didn't really mind, but I decided a golf widow I was not going to be. At the country club we joined back in Ohio I started to take golf lessons from the pro. The pro was ten years older than me and looked like Ronald Colman. When Ralph saw me taking a lesson from this gentleman, he insisted that he take over my training. He has not stopped telling me how to play golf. For forty years he tactfully reminded me to keep my head down, my left arm straight, and to follow through with my putter. But he also would wrap himself around me, the fiend, to help straighten out my slice. When we were about fifty I developed a bad hook that frequently got me into a deep rough. Ralph and I spent many a happy moment searching for my ball. Do you think it is possible to develop a hook for subconscious reasons? I mean I really like the rough.

"The only thing I never liked about Ralph's golfing was his clothing. At first he dressed like everyone else—subdued. Then his colors got brighter and brighter. Finally he wound up falling in love with slacks that looked like patchwork. I really didn't like them, but I knew he did. These pants were far out. If Joseph needed golf slacks instead of a coat he would have looked just like Ralph. I discovered after years of looking at his pants of a thousand colors that if I took off my glasses, the colors blended together. I've always been nearsighted. This helped sometimes

189

when I thought I was going to just have to tell him. Still haven't, never will.

"Anyway, I fell two years ago and broke my hip. It was a disaster. I took quite awhile to get over it. And it has meant no golf for me. Well, not exactly. You see I am the chauffeur. I usually drive Ralph in an electric cart all over the golf course. I get to tell him to keep his head down, not to bend his left arm, and to follow through when he putts."

Mildred's unfortunate accident brings us to another important anti-cancer issue for the elderly—exercise. This is a very controversial topic. It seems obvious that exercise is a very good thing for all of us. It makes sense that it should help cut down the risk of cardiovascular disorders. Since sixth-grade health classes, we have been indoctrinated to believe that exercise will prevent us from keeling over at the age of fifty. The truth seems to be that there is almost no real evidence to prove this point. I have interviewed elderly people who have exercised regularly all their lives. And I have interviewed elderly people who have exercised as much as your average boulder all of their lives. I am, however, convinced that while exercise has a very questionable role in preventing heart attack, it has a very powerful role in preventing and reversing cancers. As I have pointed out, people who get better from cancer when the doctors don't think they can always have a strong need to move. Staying in bed kills cancer patients.

Exercise is an excellent way of ridding one's self of internal carcinogens. Going for a vigorous walk, bicycling, swimming, and many other noncompetitive sports are all excellent ways of "blowing off steam." The "steam" is tension and its resultant biochemical irritants. The trouble with many Americans is that we do not know how to exercise. We call running jogging. We spend enormous amounts of money on running shoes and chic outfits. And worst of all we carry our daily high-tech, high-pressure attitudes into this realm of relaxation. Running is not enough, we have to schedule marathons. After twenty miles, the

190

average marathoner begins a self-induced cancerlike symptomatology. The body starts consuming itself as the person "hits the wall." Most of today's compulsive runners, those running more than two or three miles per session, are probably doing great harm to their joints. By the time they are as old as any of the elders I interviewed, they will probably have very unhealthy and worn knees and ankles. None of my older interviewees ever ran in a race. None of them was ever very serious about competition. And absolutely none of them ever ran twenty-six miles at one time. Most of them still go for walks, many swim, and some still ride bicycles.

They seem to recognize that serious competition is a ridiculous quest for irritation. Frequently, when questioned, they made disparaging remarks about those "young crazies" who push themselves to the limit in everything, even exercise. They may play in a tennis or golf tournament. They may be in an exercise class. But they are not feeling the tension of their grandchildren who have to look like Jane Fonda to be acceptable to themselves. They have mastered the art of having fun. If they lose they will appreciate their opponents abilities whether at chess or tennis. They are just not "uptight" people.

In those areas of the world with low cancer rates, exercise is close to universal. They do not have Nikes or Addidas. If they have heard of her, Jane Fonda is still only an actress to them. And if they can read, you can bet it will not be a book on how to exercise. They already know how. Out of necessity and sometimes choice they will simply put one foot in front of the other. They will be tied to the earth and work in the fields. These less sophisticated, "primitive" people are so much more advanced, so much saner, so much calmer than the "modern" societies.

The older couples I have spoken with have this attitude toward life. In the midst of a rushing world, an overstimulating world, and at times, an unattached world, they have maintained calm through belonging to each other. In a less pressured society, this is probably far easier to achieve. These couples and their love are truly phenomenal when we consider the social environment in which they reside.

NO ONE LIVES forever. Death is inevitable. The quality of life is really what is important. In any event, like the weather death is something people seem to complain about, but no one has been able to figure out how to change it.

While everyone must die someday, cancer is not a preferred way of departing. In societies where cancer practically never occurs and longevity far exceeds ours, death just seems to happen. Obviously everyone's heart stops when we die. I think we would all agree this is the preferable way to pass on. Most of my elderly couples will die this way. They will die with less fear and anguish. They will not have to stare death in the face. Instead it will just happen.

A surviving spouse may no longer wish to live. But survivors will also be parents, grandparents, and perhaps great-grandparents. Would the departed spouse want the survivor to leave offspring any sooner than need be? Would the departed spouse want the survivor to become reclusive and depressed? Would the departed spouse want the survivor's death to be drawn out or painfully anticipated for weeks or months?

The survivor is left with this fundamental choice—to live or to die. And the choice translates to whether the survivor will relate to others or seek isolation and depression. Mourning must be shared in order to lessen the impact. Family is vitally important to share this grief. But if family is not available, friends and neighbors must substitute.

Until we rebuild it, we must compensate for the decline of the family in our society. In grief reactions people need people. Support must not stop after the formal demonstration of mourning. It must last until the person relates without the need to be helped to do so.

Younger couples can learn what these older couples have always known. Fusional love and romance do not mix well with death. Their relationships are unique. Even as they pursued work, careers, or child rearing, their marriage remained the most important thing in their lives. These older couples also appeared to have little fear or concern about death. I have encountered far greater fears in people sixty or seventy years their juniors. The older couples recognize death is like the weather, so it's not worth worrying about. There is also a sense of fulfillment to their lives. They do not speak of what could have been. They speak of what was and will be. I came to love every one of them.

10

Conclusions

PEOPLE HAVE USED MARRIAGE and the family as the basis for survival of the species since time began. People have noticed that when one partner in a long-term marriage dies, it is not uncommon for the other to follow shortly. People have known that depression has consequences for the general health. People have known how important a sense of belonging is to feeling safe and supported. People have jokingly commented on a lack of fusional sex as the cause of crabbiness and irritability. And people have connected depression, crabbiness, and increased sensitivity with cancer. In anti-fusional marriages, statements are frequently made about a spouse's behavior that is "making me sick," "trying to kill me," or even "trying to give me cancer."

We all know everything that makes up my theory. I have stolen ideas from cultures throughout the world. This is the type of book that may have many a reader saying, "Oh, yes, I've thought of that." I'm sure you have. The trouble is it will take years of expensive research to prove or disprove these ideas. Exactly why we have to is not very clear to me since we all already know what is here. Brilliant scientists will receive millions of dollars of grant money to demonstrate "scientifically" what we already know. Perhaps this is necessary to convince some people of what is obvious. Being able to talk in technical terms seems to add credibility to almost any idea. But why wait for the scientists to catch up to the rest of us. Use this book as a reminder of what man has known for thousands of years about health and longevity.

My theory says that the aspects of the nervous system that control the immune function and the endocrine system are taught how they will respond to irritants at the very beginning of life. Because the nervous system is so easily and powerfully conditioned, this conditioning or learning will last a lifetime. But the nervous system can be reeducated. Fusional marriage is one of the best ways of changing such early learning.

In addition to the early education of the immune and endocrine systems, my theory says cancer is a multiple stage proposition. The land-mine cells or, so to speak, first-stage cells are set up in early infancy. Marriage cannot correct this tendency toward unstable genetic material. Nothing we know of can. But we can help each other have a less irritating internal biochemical environment. We can help each other have an immune system that will attack and destroy beginning stages of cancer. Fusional marriage is one of the best ways of keeping these land mines from getting tripped. Fusional marriage is one of the best ways of destroying early, perhaps undetectable, precancer or even cancer cells. However, all fusional marriage can do is significantly lower the risks. If a spouse cannot give up his or her need to always perform, to seek pressure, or to wallow in physical and chemical irritations (the sun, cigarettes, etc.) even a very fusional marriage may not be enough. Cancer can still evolve.

But fusional marriage will work most of the time. Most of the time married people outlive single people. But those single people who make it to around ninety or better are not really single. They are frequently married to a job, a cause, a place, or a thing. This job, cause, place, or thing provides at least a sense of belonging. They may have been suffragettes, teachers, physicians, or bird-

196

watchers. The important thing is that they belong. If questioned about their early childhoods, they report very positive relationships with someone—mother or surrogate. Most of us will not be fortunate enough to fall in love with our research, our job, our love for nature. Most of us will need each other. We will benefit most from each other by being in a loving relationship with our spouse.

If we can take a giant step backward in terms of marriage and the family we will be taking a giant step backward in terms of cancer rates. We can return to pre-World War II rates, if we return to a pre-World War II family structure. If we learn from "less advanced" societies, we can reduce cancer rates. The human being is a whole being with all parts interacting and mutually dependent. We must again respect the influence the mind has over the body. We must see that cancer is a life-style disorder. And, we must see that life-styles can be within our control.

The best possible examples I can give are the people of Pakistan, the Andes, and the Soviet Republic of Georgia. In the town of Vilcabamba in the Ecuadorian Andes, where Catholic baptismal records have long been kept, in 1973, out of the 819 residents, 9 were over 100 years of age. In the United States there are three centenarians per 100,000 population. What a difference! In Georgia in the Caucasus region, the rate is 39 per 100,000. In the Soviet Republic of Agerbaijan, the rate is even higher—69 per 100,000. The residents of the Caucasus are most important because they are a genetically mixed population—Turks, Armenians, Jews, Russians, Georgians, Agerbaijanis. Forget genetics as an explanation of longevity.

Diet is important, but not in ways we have been led to believe. These people regularly consume milk, cheese, and red meat. They drink considerable amounts of vodka and wine, and smoking is not at all unusual. I'm talking about people well over 120 consuming such a diet for an entire lifetime. The important thing is not what is eaten, but how it is eaten. In America we are told that men should consume 2,400 calories a day. In these areas of the world the average caloric intake is 1,800 per day.

The people exercise by walking and working over rough terrain, not running marathons. Most important, they are valued as members of their communities all their lives. The elders run the show. They are needed and belong. Soviet gerontologists have shown that life-style is what is vital for a long, cancer-free life. *Of the fifteen thousand persons older than eighty who were studied, almost everyone was married. According to the Soviet doctors, a frequent, prolonged sex life existed for all of them.* After the age of one hundred sex continues, as does meaningful contribution to the community.

Many of the Georgians, Pakistanis, and South American Indians who were asked had comments about our pitifully short life span, the traditional three score and ten years. One stated that our real problem is that people really "don't live a free life." Another said we "worry too much" and "don't do what we want." A third, who was 117, responded by stating, "Hmmm . . . too literate!"

And according to many one-hundred-year-old Soviet Georgians, *"If a man has a good and kind wife, he can easily live one hundred years." And so can she!*

198